MORE Than MEMORIES III

MASTERING THE TECHNIQUES

EDITED BY JULIE STEPHANI

© 2000 by Krause Publications

Published by

krause publications

700 East State Street • Iola, WI 54990-0001
715/445-2214 • FAX: 715/445-4087   www.krause.com

Please call or write us for our free catalog of antiques and collectibles publications. To place an order or receive our free catalog, call 800-258-0929. For editorial comment and further information, use our regular business telephone at (715) 445-2214.

Compiled by Andrea White
Design by Jan Wojtech
Photography by Ross Hubbard

Library of Congress Catalog Number: 99-67508
ISBN: 0-87341-875-1
Printed in the United States of America

The content of this book is based on the *More Than Memories* TV show produced by David Larson Productions.

Each chapter is broken into two sections: The variety of "Techniques" that can be used to achieve different creative outcomes, including "how-to" instructions and materials needed, and the "Ideas and Inspirations" section offering many examples of pages and projects to show the creative possibilities of executing those techniques. Specific materials are listed for each example, with the assumption that more supplies might be needed. As a courtesy to the reader, the following is a list of the other general supplies that were used in the various examples.

GENERAL MATERIALS LIST

Craft knife	Palette	Sponge
Fabric adhesive	Paintbrush	Straight-edge scissors
Heating tool	Ruler	Photo-safe glue

THE FOLLOWING MANUFACTURERS' PRODUCTS AND PUBLISHERS' MATERIALS HAVE BEEN USED TO CREATE THE SAMPLE ALBUM PAGES AND PROJECTS IN THIS BOOK.

Accu-Cut Shape and Letter Cutting Systems®
www.accucut.com

***Creating Keepsakes*™ Scrapbook Magazine**
www.creatingkeepsakes.com

Delta Technical Coatings, Inc.
www.DeltaCrafts.com
   Cherished Memories™ Stencils
   Cherished Memories™ Acid-Free
     Paper Paint

EK Success Ltd.
www.eksuccess.com
   Border Buddy™
   ZIG® Memory System® Markers
   ZIG® Painty®
   Stickopotamus® Stickers

Fiskars® Inc.
www.fiskars.com
   Paper Edgers, Corner Edgers, Circle
   Cutter, Personal Trimmer, Rotary Cutter,
   Photo Corners, Cutting Mat, Glue Pen

Highsmith® Inc.
www.highsmith.com

Hot Off the Press, Inc.
www.hotp.com
   Paper Pizazz™
   Punch-Outs™

Jangle™
www.JANGLE.com

Krause Publications
www.krause.com
   Arts & Crafts Magazine
   Great American Crafts Magazine
   Memory Magic Magazine

3-L® Corporation
www.3LCorp.com

Pioneer® E-Z Load Memory Albums
www.pioneerphotoalbums.com

***Memory Makers* Magazine**
www.memorymakersmagazine.com

Ticker's Stickers, Inc.
www.tickerstickers.com

INTRODUCTION

Looking through old family photos, memorabilia, and journals from the past gives a person the feeling of belonging and connects them to their family roots. Collecting and displaying these family treasures in albums is what scrapbooking is all about. The albums you create will preserve your family history for future generations.

Scrapbooking involves two main components. The first involves collecting, organizing, and storing photos, memorabilia, and writings. Most items from the past were not saved in archival-safe conditions. Often these pieces need to be rescued and sometimes even restored to preserve them for the future. Your more recent pictures of past events may also be in danger. The most important thing is to place all of these precious family mementos immediately in some type of safe containers. Then begin to organize the photos in chronological order or group the photos by families and generation.

Displaying your memory items in albums is the second phase of scrapbooking which is perhaps the most fun. This book is filled with many creative techniques to choose from when designing your pages. There are so many ways to crop and mat your photos. Specialized tools make it easier and you can choose from a wide selection of decorative paper to mix and match as you wish. Include memorabilia in the appropriate places and remember that journaling is one of the most important parts of scrapbooking, whether you are listing the facts, giving a detailed narrative, or telling a descriptive story.

Collecting and preserving photos and memorabilia is well worth the time and effort you put into it. Discovering your family roots can be an exciting connection to the past, and you will find that scrapbooking is a very enjoyable and rewarding way to preserve your unique family history for generations to come.

CONTENTS

1 ORGANIZING

The more organized you are, the more time you'll have for scrapbooking! Keep track of all your supplies, photos, and ideas, and you'll save time, money, and add more fun to creating your pages. Here are some great ideas to help you improve your organizational skills.

STORAGE & DISPLAY OPTIONS

PHOTOS

One of the first things to do with your photos is have double prints made. Most developers offer free or inexpensive double sets at the time of development. This will allow you to store your originals safely and organize your second sets of photos with your other scrapbooking supplies. To organize photos, start with the most recent and work back in time. Decide on themes for albums and group photos according to your themes. Once you've grouped your photos, store them using any of these easy methods until you are ready to place them in your scrapbooks.

DRAWER BOXES

Label the outside of the drawers by category of what's inside. Your pictures will stay organized, flat, and away from dust and moisture.

PHOTO BOXES

Most photo boxes come with dividers that can be labeled according to your preferences. Your photos will be organized and easy to find, as well as safe and dust-free. Most photo boxes are acid free, but always check to be sure. The protective structure of the box makes this a great way to store most of your pictures.

Deluxe Photo Totes from Highsmith make it easy to grab your photos to take to a cropping party.

ENVELOPES

Separate photos and store in large envelopes for easy access. This is a very inexpensive way to stay organized, but be sure the envelopes are stored flat to avoid bending photos. Keep in mind, you will often have to pull all of the photos out to find the ones you're looking for.

PLASTIC SLEEVES

If you prefer to use binders, store your photos in plastic sleeves. You will be able to see the photos without handling them, but it will be more expensive. You can write on the plastic using a permanent pen to identify the subject in each particular sleeve. If you know you're going to be using a group of photos soon, this is an easy way to keep them organized and handy by placing the sleeve in a binder along with some of the supplies you plan to use.

Plastic sleeves.

NEGATIVES

At some point, you will be searching through negatives for a particular print. To make finding that particular print easier, label negatives generally by date and event. Don't spend too much time labeling them individually, instead just note basic information about the whole roll.

PLASTIC SLEEVES

Plastic sleeves allow you to view the negatives without damaging them with scratches, fingerprints, or dust. To make identification easier, write dates and events on the plastic sleeves for a quick reference. Depending on the type of sleeve you choose, you can store them in 3-ring binders or in file folders.

CARDBOARD ENVELOPES

Leave your newest photos in the envelopes they come in from the developer. Label the outside with events and dates. You can also use these envelopes for long-term storage of duplicates that have already been placed in your memory books.

How do I store my original photos?

Mark the back of the original photo with an acid-free highlighter as a precaution, and organize by theme, person, or dates. Store original photos using any of the methods in this chapter. It's a good idea to store original photos in a different place from negatives, just to be safe.

INDEX SHEETS

Some photo labs print an index sheet at the time of developing your photos. It will show you all of the photos on one roll of film. This is a great organizational tool and time saver for finding the print you're looking for, not to mention the minimal amount of space they take up. Store all your index sheets with the matching negatives for easy identification. It will keep your photo inventory organized.

FILES

Store negatives in chronological order in labeled files. This is also an inexpensive storage option.

BOXES

Acid-free boxes are available specifically for negative storage. Since negatives are smaller, this is a great way to keep them organized without taking up a lot of space. Drawer boxes are another alternative. Label the outside of drawers by events and/or dates.

FIRE-PROOF SAFES

Store your irreplaceable negatives in a safe in your home or in a safe-deposit box in a bank.

Index Sheet. Notice the date and how each photo is numbered. Organizing your photos and negatives doesn't get much easier than this!

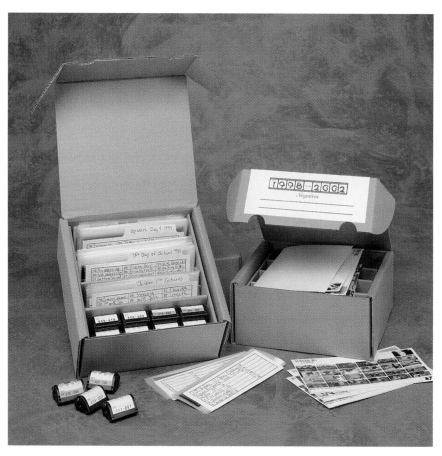

Highsmith's Negative Box. What a great way to keep negatives organized without taking up a lot of space. These are even indexed, which will save you time when looking for a particular photo.

SUPPLIES & STORAGE

The ideal way to make scrapbooking easier is to have a designated area in your home to keep all of your supplies and photos. The best for access would be shelving or closet space where you can see most things easily.

When shopping for storage for your scrapbooking supplies, don't limit yourself to scrapbooking supply stores. Check out your favorite hardware, office, and art-supply stores for everything from tackle boxes to filing supplies.

Think about what supplies you have and how you want to organize and store them. Do you travel to scrapbooking parties or classes? Do you need to move your supplies daily from one room to another? There are so many storage containers created for all kinds of different scrapbooking tools and supplies; you're sure to find the perfect storage system to fit your needs.

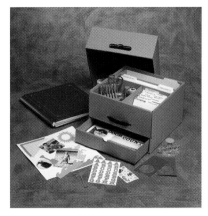

Highsmith's Speed Scrappin' Caddy is great for keeping supplies handy for the pages you're currently working on.

CLEAR BINS

Probably the simplest way to store supplies is in clear bins that can stack and store on shelves, under beds, in closets, or wherever you have room. Label the outside with the list of supplies in each particular bin. You can easily add more bins as you acquire more supplies, which you probably will.

DRAWER BOXES

Your options are endless. Decorate the box and label the drawers to make searching for supplies quick and easy. The larger boxes work great for keeping papers flat and separated by theme.

Drawer boxes are great for all supplies, especially papers, die-cuts, and stickers that you'll want to store flat. These examples are Paper Keepers from Highsmith.

PLASTIC BAGS

Keeping photos and supplies dust-free is important. Storing them in zipper plastic bags is an inexpensive way to keep things together—protected, and you can still see what's inside.

PLASTIC SLEEVES

Organizing smaller groups of items, such as stickers and die-cuts, in clear plastic sleeves will allow you to see what you have and will allow easy access to them. Place clear plastic sleeves in a binder by themes or occasions.

ALBUMS

Place items like stickers, stencils, and paper dolls in plastic sleeves and store them in albums. You might have one album for stickers, one for die-cuts, one for paper, and one for whatever projects you're working on at the time. When it's time for a cropping party, put the different sleeves for the theme you're working on in your supply album and go.

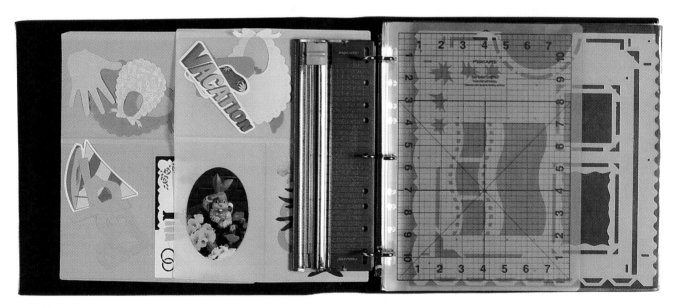

3-L's Album Organizer can hold everything from stickers to paper trimmers. This is so easy to fill with the supplies you're using on current projects. Take on an airplane or to a waiting room to work on your pages.

FILE BOXES

Stickers, die-cuts, paper, photos, and many other supplies can be organized into file folders and stored in file boxes. This will keep same items together and keep them from getting wrinkled, torn, or dusty. Another option is using hanging-file folders. Store paper labeled by type: solids, florals, contemporary, holiday themes, etc.

TOTES

There are many portable organizers available specifically designed for scrapbookers. These come in very handy if you travel often, attend cropping parties, or do a lot of your scrapbooking away from home. It's also easy to just grab a bag from the closet and take it to the table where you work.

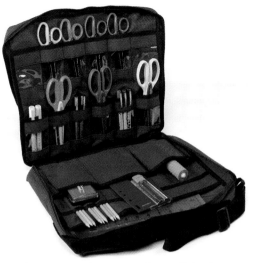

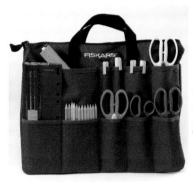

Keep a tote bag ready to go when you travel or attend cropping parties.

Fiskars' Travel Tote works well for keeping lots of supplies organized and neatly stored.

ORGANIZING ON THE PAGE

If you are concerned about your ability to create an artistic layout, don't worry. Just use these helpful tools, and your pages will look as professional as the ones you see in this book.

TEMPLATES

Templates are available for layouts as well as journaling. (See Chapter 2 for more on journaling.) After you've completed a page using your chosen papers, colors, and photos, it's hard to tell you started with a template. Don't forget, you can reverse the same template for a different look. A photo isn't the only thing you can put in each opening of a template. Add a die-cut or group of stickers in place of a photo, and you'll still achieve the balance the template is designed to create.

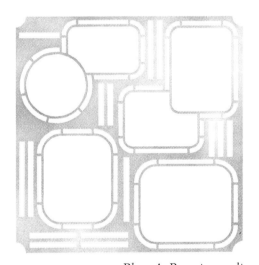

Plan-A-Page journaling templates take the work out of laying out your page. Use as a guide to plug in photos or die-cuts, and you'll have a balanced page every time.

BORROWED IDEAS

Make copies of pages and ideas that you admire. Ask friends if you can photograph their pages that you especially like. Keep a folder full of all these ideas and open it up when you need creative inspiration.

WEB SITES

Check out scrapbooking web sites. See list on page 4. You will be amazed at all of the help you can find for becoming a more organized and creative scrapbooker. Check out Jangle.com for an unending list of tips from generous scrapbookers who offer their ideas for anyone's use.

SUPPLY BOX

Design by Carol Snyder for EK Success

TECHNIQUES
Lettering
Organizing

MATERIALS
ZIG Painty Markers~
variety of colors

STAMP A GARDEN FOR STORAGE

Design by Andrea Rothenberg for Highsmith

TECHNIQUE
Stamping

MATERIALS
Highsmith Corruboard Products~Mini-Shelf and Drawers, Small Kit Storage
    Case, Magazine File
Rubber Stampede Decorative Stamps~Accent Ornate Flower, Ivy
Hot Potatoes Lower-Case Alphabet Stamps
Delta Cherished Memories Paper Paint~White, Garden Green, Red Blaze,
    Dynamo Blue, Jazzy Purple, Beach Ball, Simply Sage, Orange Sizzle,
    Raspberry Punch
Delta Cherished Memories Stencil Sponges (1 for each color paint used)
Liner paintbrush

WATCH ME GROW

Design by Toni Nelson for EK Success

TECHNIQUES
Plan-A-Page Template
Journaling

MATERIALS
Plan-A-Page~Basics #1, Rectangles #2
ZIG Memory System Markers~Fine & Chisel: Hunter Green
Paper Pizazz Papers~Gold, Rust

BASS LAKE

Design by Beth Reames for EK Success

TECHNIQUES

Borders & Corners - Template
Template - Organize your page
Journaling

MATERIALS

Plan-a-Page~Basics #1,
    Rectangles #2
Border Buddy~Beach
ZIG Memory System Markers~
    Writer: Splash, Summer Sun
    Calligraphy: Navy
Paper Pizazz Papers~Water Drop

KELSEY'S RECITAL

Design by Beth Reames for EK Success

TECHNIQUES

Borders & Corners - Template
Plan-A-Page Template
Journaling

MATERIALS

Border Buddy~Flowerfest
ZIG Memory System Markers~Fine &
    Chisel: Pure Black, Pure Pink
Plan-A-Page Templates~Basics #1,
    Rectangle #3
Paper~Pink, Black

JOURNALING

WHO, WHAT, WHEN, WHERE, WHY AND HOW

2

The photos in your albums will come to life with stories about the people and events taking place. Journaling creates a connection to the subjects, offering a glimpse into the past.

TYPE (COMPUTER)

Using a computer is certainly the easiest method of journaling. With the variety of fonts now available, you can really enhance the feel of a page. Reduce or enlarge the font to fit your space. Change colors of words and even fit journaling to a specific shape to work with your layout. When you have a lot of journaling, use the computer to make it compact and legible. Add details about what happened the day the photo was taken, or what funny thing your child said at his age in the photo. Your family will appreciate the information you give along with the pictures.

Measure the area on your page designated for your journaling. Create that same size on your computer document. Next, choose a font that will compliment the theme of your page. Use easier-to-read fonts for larger sections of words, saving the fancier typefaces for titles and short phrases.

What's great about doing your journaling on the computer is the variety of options you'll have. Adjust your lines. Add more space between lines or choose a larger type to fill up a space. Have some words in bold or italics to accentuate those words and, of course, spell-check your finished journaling. After you print the journaling, cut the edges with decorative-edged scissors, mat it, and add it to your page. With larger fonts, cut out individual letters and add to your page. Once you see how easy it is to use your computer for journaling, you'll have no excuses for not journaling on every page in your album.

HANDWRITTEN

Most of us don't like our own handwriting, but keep in mind how personal the page becomes when you include your handwriting or a relative's note or letter. You will be glad you took the time to give your memory books this personal touch. Including notes, postcards, recipes, or letters from relatives is a way to incorporate their handwriting into your family history. Ask kids to do some writing on their pages. These are the elements that create a family keepsake.

Find a comfortable place to work on your journaling. If you're using a new pen, practice before you begin. Once you've decided what you want to write, practice a few times on scratch paper before you use the card or paper you've chosen for your journaling.

Get creative with incorporating handwriting on your pages. Color copy the kids' homework and use as background paper for school pictures. Add excerpts from relatives' letters along with their pictures to add even more historical value to your memory books. How about including love letters or messages from valentines on an anniversary page? These are the things that make your books more meaningful and personal—the keepsakes your family will treasure for years to come.

Here are just a few of the many lettering ideas available, complete with how-to's and suggested uses. "Creating Letters, Borders and Doodles" booklets from EK Success are wonderful resources for inspiration.

LETTERING

There are so many creative lettering styles and techniques for us to choose from to enhance any theme. Many scrapbooking magazines and books include step-by-step instructions that show how to create unique letters and characters. If you don't have the time or patience to draw your own letters, you can trace them on your pages. Use a light table or trace on a window during daylight hours.

Box 1
Right or Left
Handed

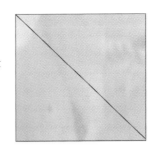
Box 2
Left
Handed

CALLIGRAPHY

Calligraphy is a great way to letter your pages. Calligraphy pens or ZIG's Scroll & Brush pens are great for learning this form of lettering. The scroll tip is the easiest to start with because the split tip helps you see if you're holding the pen correctly. Take a look at the illustration above for steps on how to hold your pen correctly. If you're right-handed, line up the tip of your pen on the lower part of the 45-degree angle in Box 1. For lefties, line up the pen tip on the top portion of the 45-degree angle, or line up your pen tip with the bottom portions of the 45-degree angle in Box 2. (The difference in the two depends on how you hold the paper.) Once you're comfortable holding the pen, practice writing zigzags, wavy lines, and then letters.

Reprinted from Quick Calligraphy published by Creating Keepsakes Magazine

STICKERS

Using stickers for words is especially fun when you have a lot to journal. Not only are the stickers fun substitutions for words, but they add an attractive embellishment to the scrapbook page. Add the stickers as you journal to assure they will fit in each sentence. Use pens to add fun accents like the cord on the Christmas light stickers or the hooks on the ornament stickers. (See Decorating at the Dayley's on page 28) It's also fun to change the color of pen to emphasize key words. Have the kids help with this—it can be a lot of fun!

STAMPING

Journaling using stamps can be lots of fun, and the outcome will be an original and creative page. There are stamps specifically for journaling with sayings and phrases, blank lines to create a neat area to journal on, or stamp characters and designs to fill in between the words for a whimsical touch to your journaling. You can color in your stamp design, then use your computer to scan and resize it if it's not quite the right size for your layout. This technique can also be used to create your own die-cuts using stamps. (See September and Corrina on page 86)

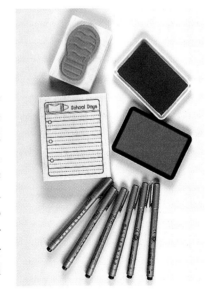

Journaling stamps are another way to keep your journaling neat and attractive by providing guidelines in a variety of patterns.

How do I come up with fun and interesting things to say on my pages?

Keep a notebook handy, and when you read a great quote or saying, write it down. There are many books available with famous and interesting quotations and anecdotes. Next time you're looking for journaling ideas, you'll have lots to choose from. Still can't think of anything to write? Ask the people in the photos what they remember from the day the photo was taken.

TEMPLATES

There are laser-cut templates designed specifically to help you with journaling. These can be used to keep paragraph widths uniform or to create straight, wavy, swirled, or curvy journaling lines. Others are different shapes to allow you to write around a photo and create a very professional looking page. Keep the overall look of the page in mind to create a balance. If your photos are small, add journaling to fill up the page, being careful not to overwhelm the photos with large embellishments.

JOURNALING BACKGROUNDS

Be creative. Let the theme of your page determine what you journal on. Write on a recipe card to go along with a photo of someone cooking. Include the floral gift card that was given with the flowers in a photo. Always check for acidity levels on these uncommon scrapbooking supplies. Reproduce non-safe items by color copying or scanning and printing. You can use die-cuts to reinforce the actions or themes, such as a football to write the score of the game or a teddy bear with the baby's birth date and weight. They're available in numerous shapes and are glued to the page around the photos. They can be cut from plain or patterned papers, then used as a base for journaling.

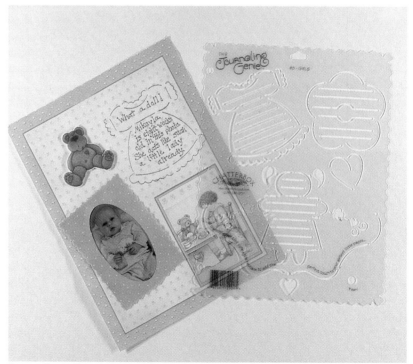

Journaling Genie from Chatterbox. Journaling templates come in many varieties and help make your handwriting look neat, professional, and more creative.

PHOTOS OF SIGNS

Don't forget to take pictures of signs when on vacation or as part of school albums. A photo of the actual sign on your album page will really bring back memories of a trip or school days and will capture valuable information for journaling. (See Graduation on page 29) Take photos of your neighborhood grocery store, favorite park sign, or the movie theater marquee—what better way to journal everyday events. These will be even more special if you happen to move. You'll have part of your history to take along with you.

When you see a great sign, take a picture.
This is such an easy way to journal
and is sure to bring back memories.

How can I include longer journaling without detracting from the photos on my page?

Here's a great trick. Cut a die-cut on a fold (like a paper doll chain), so you have multiple surfaces to pull out and journal on! Make the chain as long as you need to accommodate your journaling. You can also journal on a larger piece of paper, fold it, and place it in a pocket or envelope. You can even attach it to the back of the page and include a little note on your page that indicates there is additional journaling attached.

MY AUNTS

Design by
LeNae Gerig for Hot Off The Press

This is a photo of my aunts, Grace Marian Adams, born Feb. 8, 1904, and Iva Margaret Adams, born Oct. 16, 1908. It was probably taken in 1909. When I was little, we lived in the same small Oregon town as Aunt Iva. Most days, we went to Aunt Iva's for lunch and played with the goldfish pond in the backyard. Our families shared a cow, which we drank milk from and whose calves fed us, except for Bull Durham. Bull Durham was our favorite calf. We loved riding him around the yard. My cousins tried to play rodeo with him, but he was so tame that he would never buck. When we found out that he was in the freezer, no one would eat meat for fear of eating our old friend.

TECHNIQUES
Journaling - Computer
Punch-Outs
Photo Corners

MATERIALS
Paper Pizazz Papers~Jewel, Heavy
  Metal
Paper Pizazz Punch Outs~
  Watercolors
Pioneer Photo Corners

Emma 1919

I love these pictures of Grandma Emma as a young girl because she seems to be having such fun. If you look closely you can see someone standing behind her making her laugh.

EMMA~1919

Design by
Katie Hacker for Hot Off the Press

TECHNIQUES
Journaling - Computer
Punch-Outs
Photo Corners

MATERIALS
Paper Pizazz Papers~Hydrangeas,
  Purple Sponged
Paper Pizazz Punch-Outs~Watercolor
Pioneer Photo Corners~Silver

ENGLAND'S NARROW BOATS

Design by Julie McGuffee for Pioneer

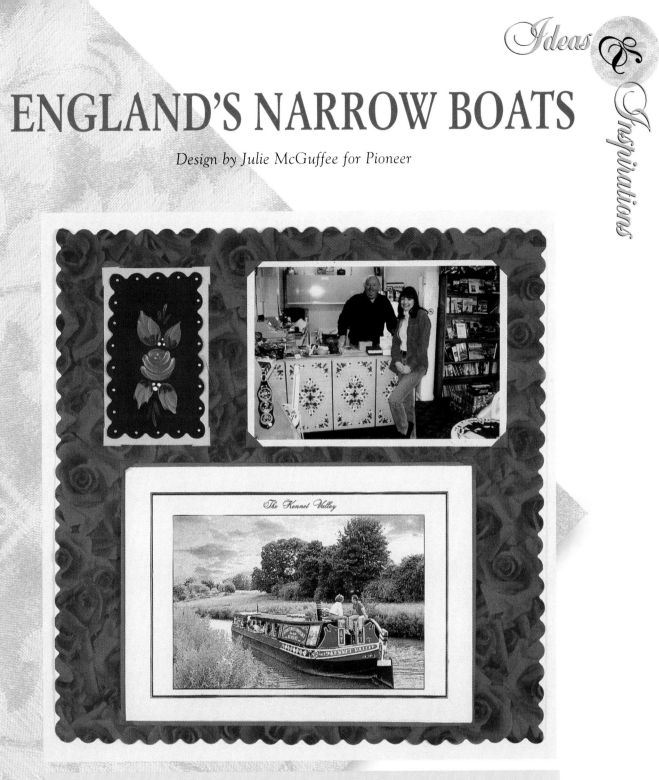

TECHNIQUES

Journaling - Done on inside of
note card
Photo Corners
Embellishing - Hand Painting

MATERIALS

Paper Pizazz Papers~Blooming
Blossoms
Pioneer Photo Corners~Rainbow
Pioneer Refill Paper~Black
Delta Paper Paint~Red, Yellow,
Green
Fiskars Paper Edgers~Cloud

BEST FRIENDS

Design by Julie McGuffee for More Than Memories

TECHNIQUE

Journaling - Lettering

MATERIALS

Pioneer Album Refill Paper

Pioneer Photo Glue Stick

Paper Pizazz Papers~Stripes, Checks and Dots;
   Solid Muted Colors

ZIG Memory System Marker~Writer: Purple

Fiskars Paper Edgers~Pinking

ON THE BORDER

Design by Julie McGuffee for More Than Memories

TECHNIQUES

Journaling - Die-Cuts, Lettering,
　　Sign Photo
Photo Corners
Borders & Corners
Punch-Outs

MATERIALS

Paper Pizazz Papers~Stripes, Checks
　　and Dots; Solid Muted Colors
Paper Pizazz Punch-Outs~Fall Leaf
Pioneer Photo Corners~Rainbow
Accu-Cut Die-Cut~Maple Leaf, small
ZIG Memory System Marker~
　　Writer: Black

DECORATING AT THE DAYLEY'S

Design by Jennie Dayley for EK Success

TECHNIQUES
Journaling - Stickers
Matting

MATERIALS
Stickopotamus Stickers~Christmas
   Accessories, Christmas Wrap,
   Santa's Workshop
ZIG Memory System Markers~Writer:
   Pure Red, Hunter Green
Paper Pizazz Papers~Holly, Plaid,
   Christmas Background

GRADUATION

Design by Julie McGuffee for Pioneer

TECHNIQUES

Journaling - Sign Photo, Adhesive Lettering
Photo Corners
Punch-Outs - Frames

MATERIALS

Pioneer Album Paper
Pioneer Photo Corners~Gold, Clear, Metallic
Pioneer Self Adhesive Letters~Gold
Paper Pizazz Papers~Pretty & Classy; Plain Pastels
Paper Pizazz Punch-Outs~Frames

GORDON IN THE SERVICE

Design by Katie Hacker for Hot Off The Press

TECHNIQUES
Journaling - Handwritten
Die-Cuts

MATERIALS
Paper Pizazz Papers~Metallic,
Jewel, Military
Accu-Cut Die Cut~Star

CRAZY QUILT ALPHABET BORDER

Design by Carol Snyder for EK Success

R Q P O N
A
M
B
L
C
K
D
J
E F G H I
A Scrapbook
is quite like a Quilt.
Each scrap addition
is lovingly gathered
piece-by piece
and stitched together
by hand and heart.
It takes time,
lots of time...
But when finished
and passed on,
the memories are there
to touch and feel again!

TECHNIQUES

Journaling - Lettering
Template

MATERIALS

Paper Pizazz Papers~White, Patterned
ZIG Memory System Markers~Writer: Black; Millennium: 05, 01, 03
EK Success Memory Pencil sets~Earth, Pastel, Primary
ABC Tracer Upper Dot Template
Fiskars Paper Edgers~Pinking

3 CREATIVE CUTTING & LAYERING

If unique is what you're looking for, this is where you can make a difference. Let your imagination go and try a few of these techniques to add originality to your pages.

CUTTING

STRAIGHT CUT

For cropping with a straight edge or pattern-edged scissors, hold the scissors still and cut while turning the photo. To improve cutting performance, cut through wax paper and aluminum foil or try rubbing an eraser over the blades. These two methods will remove paper dust particles, which can hinder a blade's performance. Here's an interesting idea: Take photos of objects like flowers, trees, nature, or interesting surfaces and cut your title's letters from those pictures for pages with an outdoor theme.

PATTERN-EDGED SCISSORS

To make the design continuous when using pattern-edged scissors, make the first cut. Realign a point or curve of the Paper Edgers blade with a corresponding point or curve of the first cut. Then make the next cut.

Use the same or different paper edgers when cutting layers of mats. Stay consistent by using one design on all of the first mats, another design on all of the second mats, etc. Choose edgers that complement your photos, using a lacy look for a feminine page, or pick up the same design that's in a photo or background paper to help tie your elements together.

Paper edgers are an easy way to add detail to a mat or border. To keep the design continuous, stop cutting before you reach the tip, realign the blade and continue your cut.

LACE EDGES

To make lace, trim the edge of the mat with paper edgers and "punch" in your lace using different sized circle hand punches. Repeat with as many mats as desired. (See Bookworms on page 50)

PAPER TRIMMER

For a clean, straight line without using a pencil and ruler, try a personal paper trimmer. They also work great for making interior cuts that scissors can't make.

CIRCLE AND OVAL CUTTER

Tracing and cutting circles and ovals can be time-consuming. The circle cutter is adjustable, allowing you to cut circles from 1" to 8". There is a needle point for precise realignment and a gripper foot for circles without pinholes. Two oval shapes, narrow and wide, can be made with the oval cutter. You can cut paper and other thin materials and put it to great use cropping photos and creating mats. When cutting photos or other important materials, cut a circle out of scrap paper first and place it over the material to be cut to make sure your measurement is correct.

SILHOUETTING

Silhouetting is cutting around the person or object. This allows the focal point of the photo to become very important on your album page. Use a sharp craft knife and mat to cut along the edge of the main subject, removing all the background. (See Grandma's Angels on page 36) Cutting a mat in the same shape as a silhouetted photo will really make this a strong element on your page.

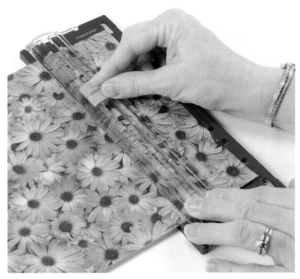

A Paper Trimmer from Fiskars is the perfect tool for straight and interior cuts.

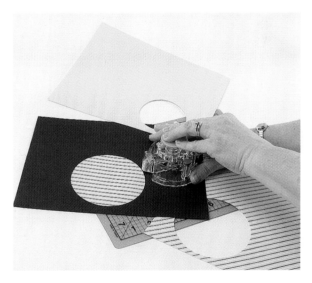

Make perfect circles every time using the Circle Cutter and Mat from Fiskars.

BUMPING OUT

Bumping out one section of the photo is silhouetting one area, but leaving the rest of the photo with a background. This cropping technique works especially well with balloons, hats, bike tires, or bent elbows. When matting a bumped-out cropped photo, it's good to keep the mat simple and cut close to the photo.

I'm afraid to cut my photos. What if I make a mistake?

You don't have to cut your priceless original photos. Free double prints are easy to find, as well as color copy machines. Computer scanners and printers can also be used to make copies of photos, even allowing you to crop, edit, and resize.

DIE-CUTS

You can find many ways to use paper cutouts on your scrapbook pages. Die-cuts come in thousands of shapes and sizes and can be cut quickly using a roller-cutting system. You can also find packaged die-cuts sold by popular themes. Use die-cuts as mats, journaling backgrounds or to enhance the theme of a page. Coordinate colors to work with your photos.

Creating your own die-cuts is also a great way to use up scraps of paper. If you can't find a ready made die-cut in the shape you're looking for, just take a look around the house. Coloring books, cookie cutters, kids' stencils, and craft books are all great sources for patterns to make your own die-cuts.

LAYERING

For a more complex look on a page, try layering elements to create a scene. Cut multiples of your desired shape with a die-cut, using different colors or prints of paper. (See The Mountains on next page) Position layers on page, overlapping layers slightly and adjusting positions until a pleasing arrangement is achieved. Trim sections apart as necessary to create interest and depth. It is easiest to start at the top of the page and build down.

TEMPLATES

Transparent plastic templates and photo stencils can be used to create perfect ovals, circles, hearts, stars, balloons, and other shapes. Position the template on top of the photo and use a very sharp pencil to mark on the photo. Then cut inside the line with straight or pattern-edged scissors.

TEARING PAPER

Using torn paper can add texture to your page. Different types of paper can determine the type of torn edge you will get. Thicker paper works best for tearing. Measure and cut the paper to the approximate size, then trace around the object with a pencil. Carefully tear, following your pencil outline. For a rough edge, hold a metal ruler along the line to be torn, swipe along the ruler with a wet paintbrush, then tear. Begin with simple shapes and work your way up to more intricate shapes. The more contrast between papers, the more you will notice the torn edge. (See Torn Paper Box on page 37)

Die-cuts come in all shapes and sizes. Use for matting, journaling, or filling in dead space.

THE MOUNTAINS

Design by Jean Kievlan for Accu-Cut

TECHNIQUE

Die-Cuts - Layering
Borders & Corners -
　Template

MATERIALS

Accu-Cut MARK IV Roller Die Cutting Machine
Accu-Cut Die-Cuts~Landscape; Mountain; Tree
　#1A, small; Clear Cut
Paper Pizazz Papers~Solid Muted Colors: Burgundy,
　Navy, Purple, Green, Yellow, Lt. Green
Border Buddy Template
ZIG Memory System Markers~Writer: Blue, Purple

GRANDMA'S ANGELS

Design by CJ Wilson for Accu-Cut

TECHNIQUES

Creative Cutting - Silhouette
Die-Cuts
Lettering

MATERIALS

Accu-Cut MARK IV Roller Die Cutting
   Machine
Accu-Cut Die-Cuts~Heart #2, large;
   Angel #1B, small
Paper~Brown, Tan
Cardstock~Maroon, Denim Blue
Parchment Paper~Tan, Pink, Light Blue
Vellum
Alphabet Letters~Gold
ZIG Memory System Markers~Writer:
   Blue, Green
Fiskars Paper Edgers~Ripple

TORN-PAPER BOX

Design by Jean Kievlan for Accu-Cut

TECHNIQUE
Cutting - Tearing

MATERIALS
Accu-Cut MARK IV Roller Die Cutting Machine
Accu-Cut Die-Cuts~Clear Cuts: Heart #5, large;
    Rectangle, large; Oval, large
Hot Off The Press Paper~Muted Pretty Paper:
    Blue/Lavender, Watercolor Floral: Hydrangea Print,
    2 of each color
Xyron 850 Machine and Adhesive Cartridge
Color Photocopies of Photos~8 of each
Octagon Paper Mache Box~5" x 8"
Sheer Ribbon~18" of 1 1/2" Green
Tulle~18" x 4" of Lt. Blue
Paper Rose Cluster~Lavender

SEWING BOX

Design by Jean Kievlan for Accu-Cut

TECHNIQUES
Die-Cut - Fabric
Photo Transfer

MATERIALS
Accu-Cut MARK IV Roller Die Cutting Machine
Accu-Cut Die-Cuts~Picture frame Oval, large;
    Heart #3, small; Mini Leaves; Flower, large
Heat'n Bond Fusible Adhesive
Photo transfer sheet
Vintage Photo
Cotton fabric~1/4 yard each
Prym-Dritz Fabric Covered Sewing Box (St. Jane
    Collection)
Buttons~7 each, 2 colors
Fancy Gold Button
10" of 1/2" ribbon

NOAH BAG

Design by Jean Kievlan for Accu-Cut

TECHNIQUES
Die-Cuts
Bag Bonnet

MATERIALS
Accu-Cut MARK IV Roller Die Cutting Machine
Accu-Cut Die-Cuts Noah's Ark #2, large; Horse,
    large; Elephant, large; Giraffe, large
Scalloped Bag Bonnet
Cardstock~Ivory
ZIG Memory System Marker~Millennium: Black 05
Xyron 850 Machine and Adhesive Cartridge
Buttons~Thirteen 3/8"
Paper Gift Bag~Burgundy
Fabric Scraps
Paper Pizazz Paper~Handmade: Ecru Print

THE APPLE OF MY EYE

Design from Fiskars, Inc.

TECHNIQUE
Borders - Paper Chain
Matting
Die-Cuts
Hand punch

MATERIALS
Fiskars Paper Edgers~Pinking, long, wide;
    Ripple, wide; Seagull, wide
Fiskars 12" Portable Paper Trimmer
Fiskars Hand Punch~Teardrop
Paper Pizazz Papers~Dots, Checks, Plaids
    & Stripes, Plain Pastels
Accu-Cut Die-Cuts~Circles
Fiskars Photo Stickers

BUNDLED UP

Design from Fiskars, Inc.

TECHNIQUES
Matting
Cutting - Paper Trimmer

MATERIALS
Fiskars Paper Trimmer
Fiskars Corner Edgers~Rounder
Fiskars Photo Stickers
Paper Pizazz Papers

MORGAN JONES

Design by Melodie Jones for Hot Off The Press

TECHNIQUES
Punch-Outs
Scrapliqúe

MATERIALS
Paper Pizazz Papers~Country: Barnwood,
    Denim; Solid Plain Brights: Red, Green,
    Orange; Solid Muteds: Dark Brown,
    Brown
ZIG Memory System Markers~Brown, Gold

BORN TO CAUSE TROUBLE

Design by LeNae Gerig for Hot Off the Press

TECHNIQUES
Matting
Journaling - Lettering
Punch-Outs

MATERIALS
Paper Pizazz Papers~Textured: Leathers;
    Solid Jewel Tones: Brown, Black
Fiskars Paper Edgers~Alligator
Punch-Outs~Sayings

TREASURED PIECES

Design by Eileen Ruscetta for Memory Makers

Treasured pieces of Ashton's Life

TECHNIQUES
Creative Cutting - Template
Journaling
Matting

MATERIALS
Paper Pizazz Papers~of your choice
Fiskars Hexagon Template
Fiskars Swivel Knife

ANNALISE

Design by Susan Cobb for Hot Off The Press

TECHNIQUES
Die Cuts
Punch-Outs

MATERIALS
Paper Pizazz Papers~Paper Quilting: Blue
    Plaid, Pastel Dot, Pink Dot, Pastel
    Stripe, Pastel Hearts on yellow; Solid
    Pastels
Accu-Cut Die-Cut~Teddy Bear
Fiskars Paper Edgers~Scallops
ZIG Memory System Markers
Fiskars Heart Punch

ME & MY GUYS

Design by Katie Hacker for Hot Off The Press

TECHNIQUES
Matting
Cutting - Circle, Oval
Journaling

MATERIALS
Paper Pizazz Papers~Bright Great Backgrounds: Tie
  Dye, Purple Chalky, Magic Stones, Green
  Swizzle, Blue Tiles; Solid Jewel Tones: Black
Fiskars Paper Edgers~Deckle
Handmade Whale Pattern
ZIG Memory System Marker~Black

RUBBER DUCK

Design by Cathie Allan for Memory Makers

TECHNIQUES	MATERIALS
Matting - Silhouette	Paper Pizazz Papers~White,
Stamping	Turquoise, Yellow, Orange
Dimensional dots	Stamps~Bubble in desired sizes
Journaling	Rubber Stamping Markers~varying
	shades of blue
	Corner rounder punch
	Dimensional dots

FLORIDA KEYS

Design by Julie McGuffee for Accu-Cut

TECHNIQUES
Die-Cuts
Paper Trimmer
Stickers
Lettering
Cutting - Silhouetting

MATERIALS
Accu-Cut Die-Cuts~Beach landscape, Wave border
Paper Pizazz Papers~Pastel, Jewel Tones
Fiskars Personal Paper Trimmer, Scissors
ZIG Memory System Marker~Writer: Black
Stickopotamus Stickers~Beach, Tropical Fish
Chalk~Light Orange Pastel
Small Stencil Brush

BORDERS & CORNERS

Making easy yet creative borders & corners can be the difference between an average album page and one with pizazz!

MATTING

Mat your images to create a visual separation between the image and the background. You can use pre-cut mats, use punch-outs or die-cuts, make your own—the list goes on and on. Nothing groups photos together like coordinating frames and papers to carry the theme through the whole page. The possibilities are endless, but you'll want to keep a few suggestions in mind:

•Create a visual separation between the image and the background. Solids are typically best for this.

•Overlap the pieces to pull your eye through all elements of the page.

•Keep the lettering and mats simple to allow the photos to stand out.

•Put a photo at an angle to break the pattern slightly which is more pleasing to the eye.

•Cut the mats with a decorative edge to pick up the details of the background paper which adds to the professional look of a page.

SHADOWING

"Shadowing" is creating a mat which matches the shape of the matted item, but is placed offset behind the shape. To get a true shadow effect, it's important to place the mats in the same relative position for each element, as though each is lighted from the same source. To shadow an irregular shape, lay the matted shape upside down on the wrong side of the shadow color. Trace it lightly, then cut around the pencil line and turn the mat over.

OFFSET MATS

A mat doesn't have to be an even border all around the edge of a photo, and a background paper doesn't have to sit straight on the page. Offsetting one or more mats, and background papers adds interest to your pages. An offset mat can emphasize an especially rich paper.

BRAIDING

To create a decorative border, cut two narrow strips with wide paper edgers of your choice and weave the strips together. Position and glue to background paper. (See Bookworms on page 50, and top border of Apple of My Eye on page 38)

Notice how the white mat pulls the photo out away from the floral background paper. The colored photo corners are a great way to tie the photo to the floral background as well as the solid background.

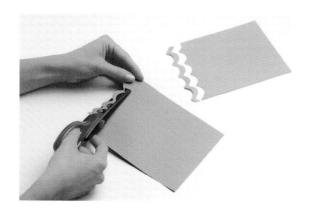

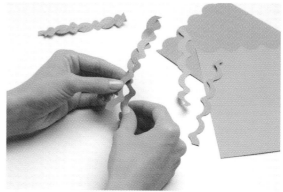

PAPER CHAINS

With the variety of scissors available, you can make a different border every time. (See bottom border of Apple of My Eye on page 38)

A Fold the paper in half the long way.

B Choose the most protruding part of the blade design, realign, and consistently cut little bites out of fold with that part of the blade for a perfect chain. Using more or less of the blade design will alter the paper chain pattern, making it irregular.

C Position the blade on the fold so that only part of fold is cut. Like a snowflake, part of the folded edge has to be left uncut. Cut to the end of the folded strip.

D Flip paper over and cut parallel to folded edge. Open up folded paper.

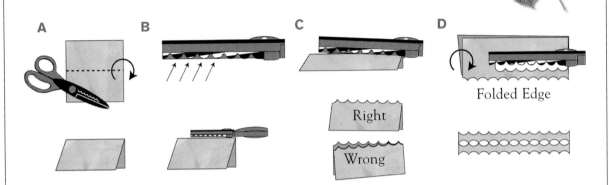

Reprinted from Fiskars Paper Edgers Tips

TEMPLATES

Many borders and design elements can be created using templates. Use them to make creative page borders and decorative edges. Use templates to stencil and add embellishments. They come in an assortment of bordering patterns and fancy corners. They are made from see-through plastic for ease in placement and feature marker holes for alignment and page positioning.

Using a Border Buddy template keeps your page unique and professional looking.

CORNERS

PHOTO CORNERS

Photo corners are a practical creative accent. Using corners to mount your photos will give you the ability to remove your photos easily. Add corners to mats and borders to add flair to a page without covering up the images.

Draw, write, or paint on the corners to make them even more unique. Color white photo corners with markers to coordinate with your layout.

Photo Corners come in clear, black, white, silver, and gold, as well as rainbow assortments. They are archival safe and self-adhesive—no more licking and sticking.

Score along lines. Cut bottom edge with Paper Edgers. Fold corners under. Slip corners onto photo and glue on page. (See A Shave and a Haircut on page 52)

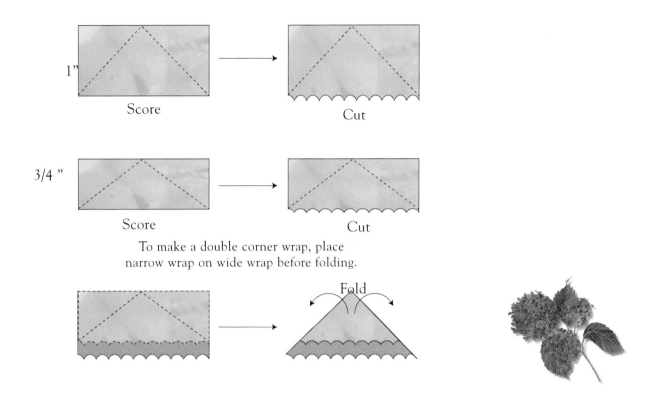

1"

Score   Cut

3/4"

Score   Cut

To make a double corner wrap, place
narrow wrap on wide wrap before folding.

Fold

How do I get the design to come out even at the corners
when I use paper edgers?

A - To create a mat that has perfect, identical corners, cut a strip of paper to make a template for each design. Position this template on the edge of the photo and line up design to be the same on each corner of the photo so corners are identical. Hold securely in place and use as a cutting guide.

B - Each time you create a new template with a different paper edger, add it to a ring. Soon you will have all of them.

C - By using this method, you can make perfect corners every time.

A   B   C

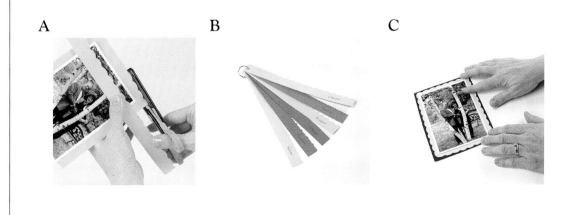

BOOKWORMS

Design from Fiskars, Inc.

TECHNIQUES
Matting
Cutting - Lace
Borders - Braiding

MATERIALS
Fiskars:
  Hand Punches~1/16" circle, 1/8"
    circle, 1/4" circle
  Paper Edgers~Seagull, Seagull, wide
  Corner Edgers~Rounder
  Portable Paper Trimmer
Paper Pizazz Papers~Black & White
    Photos, Plain Pastels

SPINACH AGAIN?

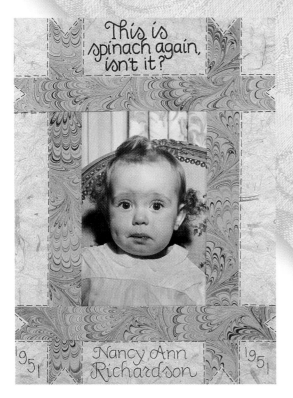

Design by Carol Snyder for EK Success

TECHNIQUES
Journaling - Lettering
Borders & Corners
Photo Tinting

MATERIALS
Paper Pizazz Papers~Plain Pastels:
    Beige; Patterned Paper: Brown
ZIG Photo Twin markers for photo
    tinting
ZIG Memory System Marker~Writer:
    Black

A VERY MERRY CHRISTMAS

Design by Beth Reames for EK Success

TECHNIQUES

Borders & Corners - Template
Embossing - Markers
Template - Organize Your Page
Journaling

MATERIALS

Border Buddy~Winter
ZIG Memory System:
    Markers~Writer: Spice, Hunter
        Green; Fine & Chisel: Hunter Green
    Embossing Markers~Fine & Chisel:
        Hunter Green
    Embossing Powder~White
Plan-A-Page Basics~#1, Rectangles #2

A SHAVE AND A HAIR CUT

Design by Sandra Cashman for Fiskars

TECHNIQUES
Matting
Corner Wraps
Die-Cuts

MATERIALS
Fiskars:
 Corner Edgers~Rounder
 Paper Edgers~Seagull
 Micro-Tip Scissors
 Portable Paper Trimmer
Accu-Cut Die-Cuts~Circle
Paper Pizazz Papers~Book of Firsts,
 Plain Brights, HoHoHo

LOOK MOM, TWO WHEELS!

Design by Beth Reames for EK Success

TECHNIQUES
Border & Corners Template
Template - Organize Your Page
Journaling

MATERIALS
Plan-A-Page Jr.~Jr. Basics #1, Squares #1
Border Buddy Jr.~Hearts and Bows
ZIG Memory System Markers~Writer:
 Pure Violet; Fine & Chisel:
 Pure Pink
Paper Pizazz Papers~Solid Brights

A TOUCH OF COLOR AT EASTER

Design by Carol Snyder for EK Success

TECHNIQUES
Matting
Photo Corners
Photo Tinting

MATERIAL
Paper Pizazz Papers~Solids: Black; Pretty Papers:
    Green Marble
ZIG Memory System Markers~Opaque Writer:
    Fine White; Millennium 03
ZIG Photo Twin Markers for photo tinting
Fiskars Paper Edgers~Pinking
Photo Corners

A STAR IS BORN

Design by Toni Nelson for EK Success

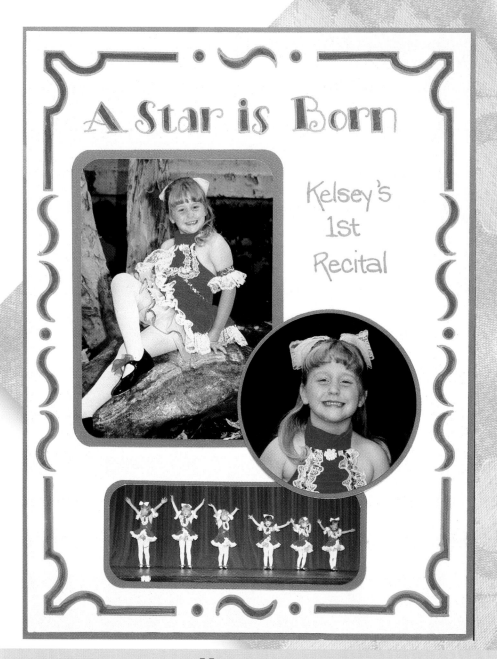

TECHNIQUES

Borders & Corners -
Template Lettering

MATERIALS

Border Buddy Jr.~Reflections, Victorian
ZIG Memory System Markers~Writer:
    Pure Pink; Opaque Writer: Gold,
    extra fine
Paper Pizazz Papers~Gold
Fiskars Paper Trimmer

O CHRISTMAS TREE

Design by Toni Nelson for EK Success

TECHNIQUES

Borders & Corners -
    Template
Cutting - Silhouette
Journaling

MATERIALS

Border Buddy~Winter
ZIG Memory System Markers~Scroll
    and Brush: Hunter Green; Writer:
    Chocolate, Hunter Green
Paper Pizazz Papers~Hunter Green

GIRLS IN THE GARDEN

Design by Toni Nelson for EK Success

TECHNIQUES
Borders & Corners - Template
Embossing - Markers

MATERIALS
Border Buddy~Flowerfest
ZIG Embossing Markers~Writer: Candy
    Pink, Lavender, Bluebonnet;
    Calligraphy: Lavender
Embossing Powder~Yellow
Paper Pizazz Papers~Solid Brights

JAKOB
AT THE LAKE

Design by Bernice Wery for Hot Off The Press

TECHNIQUES
Punch-Outs - Frames
Journaling

MATERIALS
Paper Pizazz Papers~Dots, Checks Plaids
 & Stripe: Dots
Paper Pizazz Punch-Out~Frames
ZIG Memory System Markers~Writer;
 Calligraphy

ALEXANDRA

Design by Katie Hacker for Hot Off The Press

TECHNIQUES
Punch-Outs - Frames
Journaling

MATERIALS
Paper Pizazz Papers~Watercolor Florals:
 Purple Pansies; Pastel Solids: Yellow;
 Muted Solids: Purple
Paper Pizazz Punch-Outs~Childhood
 Frames
Fiskars Paper Edgers~Wave
ZIG Memory System Markers~Writer;
 Scroll & Brush

4th OF JULY

Design by Katie Hacker for Hot Off The Press

TECHNIQUES
Journaling~Stickers
Punch-Outs~Frames

MATERIALS
Paper Pizazz Papers~Dots, Checks, Plaids
    & Stripe: Navy Pinstripe
Paper Pizazz Punch-Outs~Celebration
    Frames
Letter Stickers

3-DIMENSIONAL PROJECTS 5

Add a little dimension to your pages by trying a few of these truly creative techniques!

SIMPLE TECHNIQUES

- Curl edges of die-cuts or cut-outs away from the page to add dimension.
- Use stacker stamps to create a small design. Cut out. Add a little magic by hinging two cut-outs together and gluing a small trinket inside. (See Ship Into the Past on page 79)
- Adding pressed flowers to a page adds texture and dimension. Why not add real flowers, seeds, or plants to a theme of working in the garden or on the farm? (See Garden Window Card on page 64)

DIE-CUTS

   Choose a die-cut to go with your theme and layer it or fold it to add dimension. To make flowers dimensional, fold the flower in half. Apply glue to the fold and glue it to another flower of the same color, matching the shape. Add a second folded flower in the center. Repeat for all flowers you wish to have dimension. Use any dies, such as dogs or cars or trains instead of flowers. (See Happy Memories Storage Box on page 102)

POP-UPS

If you really want to make a statement with a photo, attach it to a pop-up. Pop-ups are easy to create, once you understand how they work. In order for the image to "pop", it needs to be attached to a base with a hinge; a card with a center fold. The hinge is glued across two pages. Purchase bases and add photos and die-cuts, or create your own base with card-stock.

Attach decorative die-cuts, photos or even journaling to a pop-up base.

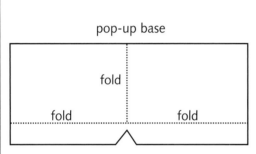

Cut a base from heavyweight paper using the pattern shown.

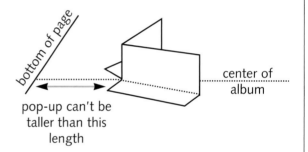

Fold the basic shape in half. Fold the bottom edges upwards toward the outside. Glue the bottom edges on your scrapbook pages on either side of the center. Glue photographs, die-cut shapes, punch outs, etc. onto the base, above the fold line. Don't make the height of the pop-up taller than the length of the page from the bottom edge to the center fold of the pop-up base.

LAYERING

Creating several independent layers and cleverly attaching them makes a fun dimensional card. Layers can be attached in the folds of an accordion fold. (See 3D Beach Scene on page 67) Another way to create dimension is by layering several die-cuts or shapes almost on top of each other. Use dimensional dots between layers to add more depth.

DIMENSIONAL DOTS

Create a 3-D effect with ease. Simply affix a dimensional dot to a die-cut or stamped image and apply wherever you would like to add depth to your project. Use one, two, or even three double-stick dots to add dimension to your pages.

To create dimensional flowers, (See Floral Fun Gift Bag on page 65) decide which flowers will be dimensional. Add a foam dimensional dot to the center of those flowers. Before adding the second flower on the dot, curl the petals around a pencil to make them a bit rounded.

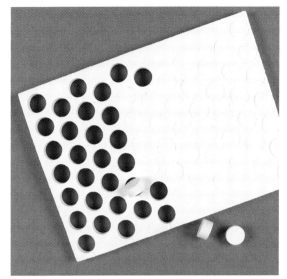

Dimensional dots are a fun and easy way to add dimension to your pages.

ACCORDION-FOLD

An easy way to add dimension is by creating a fan-fold between two layers. Do this to have a cropped image spring from the page or to create a window effect. (See 3D Beach Scene on page 67) For the window effect, take two 5" x 7" pieces of cardstock and fold each into paper fans with 1/4 inch between each fold. Place base paper horizontally and glue the first fold of one fan to the left side of the base, and the second paper fan to the right side of the base in the same manner. Attach cropped photos to an accordion fold die-cut for a unique animated presentation.

INSERTS

Adding some sort of a pull-out insert is a fun way to create action on your scrapbook pages. Include journaling or additional photos on the insert to give it a practical use, as well as a fun embellishment. Attach heavier paper to the page to use as a pocket for your insert and add a shape or lettering to the pull so people know there's more to see. (See Raise the Woof on page 66)

BAG BONNET

Why not make your next gift bag a creative and handmade one? A bag bonnet is simply a folded card with a slit in the fold for the handle of the gift bag to slide through. Embellish the bonnet with photos, ribbons, and die-cuts, etc. (See Angel Gift Bag on page 65)

RED PEPPER CARD

Design by Amy Brennan for Memory Magic

TECHNIQUES	MATERIALS
Cutting - Silhouette	Accu-Cut MARK IV Roller Die Cutting Machine
Die-cuts	Accu-Cut Die-cuts~Pop-up, small; Chili Pepper, large
Journaling	Mirricard Paper~Red, Green
	Chromolux Paper~Red, Green
	Cardstock~Red, Green, White, Tan
	ZIG Memory System Marker~Millennium: Black

ROMANTIC PHOTO CARD

Design by CJ Wilson for Accu-Cut

TECHNIQUES
Die-Cut
Embellishing

MATERIALS
Accu-Cut MARK IV Roller Die
    Cutting Machine
Accu-Cut Die-Cuts~Deckle Oval Note
    Card, jumbo; Classic Card
    Envelope A6, jumbo; Leaves, mini;
    Clear Cut Oval, large
Xyron 850 Machine

Xyron 853 Adhesive Cartridge
ZIG Memory System Markers~Opaque
    Writer: Gold, medium
Cardstock~Pastel Pink
Paper Pizazz Papers~Cream Roses,
    Green Pinstripe, Green Marble
Rose charms

TEAPOT FRAME

Design by Julie McGuffee for More than Memories

TECHNIQUES
Dimensional - Layering
Die-Cuts
Embellish - Chalk Painting
Embossing - Pressure

MATERIALS
Ready-to-Make Single Frame
Posterboard~White
Cardstock~Yellow, Pink, Pale Green
Accu-Cut Die-Cuts~Teapot, Mini Leaf, Circle
ZIG Memory System Markers~Millennium: Black 05
Pastel Chalks
Fiskars Circle Punch
Small Stencil Brush

GARDEN WINDOW CARD

Design by Linda Ullrich for Accu-Cut

TECHNIQUES

Textures - Embossing
Die-Cut
Stamping

MATERIALS

Accu-Cut MARK IV Roller Die Cutting Machine
Accu-Cut Window Notecard #2
Accu-Cut Die-Cuts~Leaf Maple #1, small; Leaves
    Jungle, small
Halo's Rubber Stamp Starter set
Cardstock~Pumpkin, Forest Green
Ink pads~Green, Burgundy
Embossing Ink~Clear
Embossing Powder~Gold
Rubber Stamp~Flower
Dried plants, flowers, or seeds

ANGEL GIFT BAG & CARD

Design by Jean Kievlan for Accu-Cut

TECHNIQUES
Die-Cuts
Bag Bonnet
Embellishments

MATERIALS
Accu-Cut MARK IV Roller Die Cutting
    Machine
Accu-Cut Die-Cuts~Star Frame, small;
    Scalloped Bag Bonnet; Heart #3, large;
    Classic Notecard; Scalloped Notecard
Paper Pizazz Papers~Pretty Papers: Yellow
    Rose Print, Blue and Yellow Rose Print;
    Solids: Blue
Cardstock~White
Xyron 850 Machine and Adhesive Cartridge
DMD Lt. Green Gift Bag with Handles
Chenille Stem~Gold Metallic, 8" Piece
Button~White or Cream, 5/8"
Gold Metallic Ribbon with Wired Edge~One Yard of 3/8"
ZIG Memory System Markers~Writer: Black, Green; Millennium: Black 03

FLORA GIFT BAG

Design by Andrea Rothenberg for Highsmith

TECHNIQUES
Dimensional - Dots
Stamping
Embellishing

MATERIALS
Highsmith Corruboard Small Gift Bag~Green
Rubber Stamps~Flower, Leaf Heart
Ink Pad~Black
Cardstock~Assorted bright colors
Dimensional dots

RAISE THE WOOF PARTY

Design from Fiskars, Inc.

TECHNIQUES
Cutting - Die-Cut
Lettering
Dimension - Insert

MATERIALS
Fiskars:
  Paper Edgers~Deckle, Stamp, Pinking
  Corner Edgers~Rounder
  12" Portable Paper Trimmer
  Photo Stickers and 2-way glue stick
Paper Pizazz Papers~Pets, Brights
Accu-Cut Die-Cuts~Lettering
ZIG Memory System Marker~Black

3-D BEACH SCENE

Design by Jennie Dayley for EK Success

TECHNIQUES
Dimension - Fan Fold
Dimension - Layers with stickers

MATERIALS
Stickopotamus Stickers~Paradise, Marine
  Animal, Beach, Shore
Cardstock~Blue
Handmade Paper~Tan
Paper Pizazz Papers~Sky, Great Background

PAPER DOLL FAMILY POP UP

Design by Jill Rinner for Accu-Cut

TECHNIQUES

Pop-Ups
Die-Cuts
Paper Dolls

MATERIALS

Accu-Cut MARK IV Roller Die Cutting Machine
Accu-Cut Die-Cuts~Pop-Up Page, medium-
	jumbo; Tree, large; Jill's Paper Doll, large
Jill's Paper Doll Clothes Dies~Various
Jill's Chunky Alphabet~Upper Case, 1 1/4"
Cardstock~Beige, Flesh, Hunter Green (two
	shades), Soft Blue

SNYDERS 1999

Design by Carol Snyder for EK Success

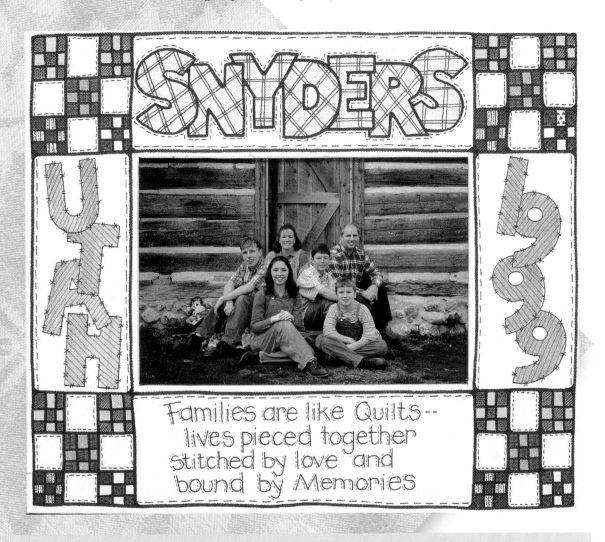

TECHNIQUES

Journaling

Lettering - Template

MATERIALS

EK Success ABC Tracers~Block

EK Success Ready-to-make 8" x 10" frame

ZIG Memory System Markers~Writer:
Black; Scroll & Brush: Pure Yellow,
Pure Green, Pure Blue, Powder Blue;
Millennium: Black 01, 03

6 CREATING TEXTURES

Take scrapbooking to a new level by adding textures to your pages to accent your photos.

PROTECT YOUR PHOTOS

Whatever materials you decide to use to add texture to your scrapbook pages, check to see if they are archivally safe. If they are not, make sure you protect your photos from touching them.

SEWING & QUILTING

It's easy to duplicate the look of sewing and quilting in your memory crafting. By drawing "stitching lines" with pens and using quilt shapes for backgrounds, create your own quilted looks on your pages. Decorate album covers using fabric appliqués, buttons, and ribbon for decoration.

SCRAPLIQUÉ

Die-cuts can also be used to create appliqué-like embellishments. Design your own pages with themes and colors to match the photos. Add stitching lines to give the feel of sewing or quilting. (See Morgan Jones on page 40)

CRIMPING

Paper crimpers quickly create a unique "ripple" or "corrugated" effect and are very easy to use. Some elements of a page are obvious choices for crimping. Use a paper crimper to add texture to grass, French fries, a paper doll's hair, or a rooftop. You'll bring your page to life. (See Let's Eat on page 82)

Crimping mats or die-cuts adds texture and interest to your page.

EMBOSSING

Embossed papers are available in many colors and designs.

EMBOSSED PAPER

One of the simplest ways to add a textured look is simply to purchase background papers that look embossed. They come in a variety of colors, designs, and themes. Use the faux embossed papers to add an elegant touch to a wedding page.

STENCIL EMBOSSING

Stencil embossing is creating a raised surface on paper using a template/stencil and an embossing stylus. This inexpensive technique for creating embossed designs can be used for any style page, from traditional to cute and whimsical. Use removable tape to position the embossing template where you want to create your design. Turn the paper over, place it on a light table, and use the embossing stylus like a pencil to trace the inside edges of the stencil. Medium-weight, light-colored papers work best for embossing. (See Forest Home on page 75)

The die-cut machine also has a Roller Embossing System which can be used for pressure embossing. (See Teddy Baby on page 87)

THERMAL EMBOSSING

Embossing with heat creates texture on a memory album page. Interesting raised effects are possible with embossing inks and powders. The heat source melts the powder and creates a raised, shiny surface. It's quite simple to emboss using an embossing writer. Just fill in desired area, using an embossing writer, pour on embossing powder, shake off excess, and heat. (See Happy Holidays Card on page 87)

Another method for embossing is to use stamps. Stamp the design using clear embossing ink or pigment ink, depending on the effect you want to create. Cover the stamped image with embossing powder which sticks to the stamped areas. Tap off loose powder. Apply heat with an embossing heat tool. A hot plate or iron will also work, but you must place these under the paper and use caution to not burn the paper. Try different stamps and colors to create unique effects.

Fiskars Brayer Backgrounds have interchangeable rollers that come in six unique designs and create cool patterns up to 6" wide.

BRAYER BASICS

Spin out unique effects on papers with a brayer and ink. There are various designs to use as backgrounds for your scrapbooking pages. Dye ink pads are acid-free, fade resistant, and fast drying. Patterns include stars, speckle, mesh, hearts and streamers, along with six dye ink pad colors to choose from. This is a sure way to keep your pages original. (See Fall Leaves on page 88)

FABRIC

Fabric die-cuts work great for embellishing the outside of photo albums or projects. Choose colors and prints to complete your theme: pastel nursery prints for baby albums or beautiful floral silks for a wedding book. (See Bunny Album on page 80 and Sewing Box on page 37)

PHOTO TRANSFER

Following instructions on package, photocopy on transfer paper. Iron fusible interfacing to one side of muslin fabric. Iron the photo transfer onto the other side of the fabric. Carefully peel away the transfer paper, making sure photo has transferred to fabric. Iron fusible interfacing onto wrong side of the other fabrics.

FAUX TEXTURES

Using sponges to paint on faux finishes can add an interesting texture to your pages and projects. Add texture to a picture frame or keepsake box with a faux finish to give it an aged look. Use paint and crackle medium to give a box or frame an antique look. (See Military Memories Shadowbox on page 107)

Is it okay to use rubber stamps and ink on my scrapbook pages?
The rubber part of the rubber stamp is neither acidic nor pH neutral. Dye-based inks dry quickly and soak down into the paper. Look for "acid-free," "photo-safe," or "archival-quality" terms on the labels of the dye-based inks. Water-based inks may bleed or eventually fade.

STAMPING

SIMPLE STAMPING

Tap the stamp on the ink pad until entire image area is evenly inked. Press the stamp down on paper or fabric using even pressure. Avoid rocking the stamp or pressing extremely hard because these movements will blur the image. Lift the stamp straight off the paper holding the paper down with one hand while lifting the stamp off the page. Allow the ink to dry. Pigment ink pads are recommended for scrapbooking because they are acid-free, permanent, and more colorfast than standard dye-based ink pads.

STAMPING WITH MARKERS

Another way to ink a stamp is by drawing directly on the raised rubber surface with markers. Color the same stamp in a variety of color combinations and create a different effect with each impression. Use light colors first to avoid getting a darker color on your lighter markers. Clean your marker by rubbing it on scrap paper. Because the ink from markers dries faster on rubber stamps, you may need to "huff" on the stamp to moisten the ink a little. Make sure you are using water-based markers; permanent markers will ruin your stamps.

STAMPING WITH PAINT

Squirt out some of the chosen paints onto your palette. Dab a sponge into each color. Blot off the excess paint. Dab each of the paints onto the stamp, covering the design completely. Practice stamping the design on paper or cardboard to get the desired look. Begin stamping the design on your project. Apply more paint after each stamp. With some designs, such as flowers or leaves, be sure to turn the stamp in different directions every time you stamp, so that the design will look more natural.

MAKING STAMPS FROM DIE-CUTS

Create your own stamps using a die-cutting machine, die-cuts and a rubber stamp starter set. The stamps can be cut the same way you would cut dies from paper. The rest is the same, just choose your color of ink or paint and start stamping! (See Henry Doorly Zoo on page 85)

Create unique stamped designs with Fiskars' Stacker Stamps and Rainbow Pad.

What are the basic things I need to know about stamping?

- Stamp on a smooth, flat surface.
- Protect other areas of your page by covering with paper.
- Practice your stamp before stamping it on the page.
- Test stamp often and re-ink the pad when necessary.
- Always clean stamps after each use and when changing colors of ink or paint.

73

Place foil over adhesive design.

Press lightly with fingers.

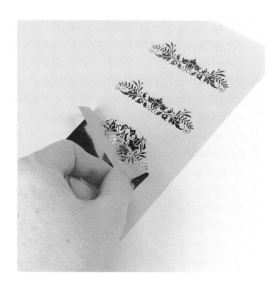

Peel foil off adhesive.

STENCILING

Stenciling can be used on paper, wood, fabric, and other paintable surfaces. Stencil with paint, oil sticks, and foil. There probably isn't a design or character that hasn't been made into a stencil, giving you endless possibilities for unique pages.

SPONGE STENCILING

Be sure to use acid-free paints when stenciling on your pages. Delta's Cherished Memories Acid-Free Paper Paint is a stencil paint specifically for scrapbooking. When stenciling on delicate surfaces such as paper, press the adhesive-backed stencils repeatedly against fabric to collect lint and lessen tack.

STENCILING WITH FOIL (See photos)

To get a very sophisticated look, use foil for your stenciling. Metallics are very popular right now and can add a dramatic look to a page or project.

When using foil adhesives, always apply two coats of adhesive. Let the first coat dry until it turns clear before applying the second coat. For best results, brush on each coat in a different direction. When using foil on surfaces with intricate detail, use an old toothbrush to rub the foil into the cracks and crevices. (See Monogrammed Wedding Frame on page 84)

FOREST HOME

Design by Toni Nelson for EK Success

TECHNIQUES

Embossing - Pressure
Dimension - Dots

MATERIALS

Border Buddy~Winter
Pebbles Tracers~Log Cabin
Embossing Stylus
ZIG Memory System Markers~Writer:
    Hunter Green
Cardstock~Hunter Green, Brown
Dimensional Dots

OH SNOW

Design by Beth Reames for EK Success

TECHNIQUES

Embossing - Pressure
Template - Organize
    Your Page
Lettering

MATERIALS

Border Buddy~Winter
Embossing Stylus
ZIG Memory System Markers~Fine & Chisel:
    Navy Blue
Plan-A-Page Jr.~Basics #1, Rectangles #1

"MOLLY"

Design by
LeNae Gerig for Hot Off The Press

TECHNIQUES
Textures - Embossed Papers
Die-Cuts

MATERIALS
Paper Pizazz Papers~Lovely & Lacy:
    Lace, Dots; Plain Pastels: White
Accu-Cut Die-Cuts~Rattle
Fiskars Paper Edgers~Ripple
ZIG Memory System Markers~Writer

MOTHER'S DAY

Design by
LeNae Gerig for Hot Off The Press

TECHNIQUES
Textures - Embossed Paper
Journaling
Matting
Punches

MATERIALS
Paper Pizazz Papers~Embossed: Mom,
    Mother, Mama; Solid Muted
Fiskars Paper Edgers~Colonial
ZIG Memory System Marker~White
Heart Punch

SPECIAL MEMORIES

Design by Becky Goughnour for Hot Off The Press

TECHNIQUES	MATERIALS
Textures - Embossed Papers	Paper Pizazz Embossed Papers~Gold, White
Matting	Paper Pizazz Papers~Metallics: Light and Dark Gold; Plain Pastels: White
Journaling - Calligraphy	Fiskars Paper Edgers~Victorian
Punches	ZIG Memory System Marker~Calligraphy
	Fleur-de-lis Punch

A SHIP FROM THE PAST

Design from Fiskars, Inc.

TECHNIQUES

Creative Cutting
Journaling
Matting
Textures - Stamping,
   Embellishments

MATERIALS

Fiskars:
   Paper Edgers~Scallop; Wave, wide
   Corner Edgers~Blossom
   Stacker Stamp~Scallop Shell
   Ink Pad~Rainbow Pigment
ZIG Memory System Marker~Black
Paper Pizazz Papers~Vacation, Plain Pastels
Pearl

BUNNY ALBUM

Design by Jean Kievlan for Accu-Cut

TECHNIQUES

Die-Cut - Fabric
Lettering
Textures - Embellishment, Fabric

MATERIALS

Accu-Cut MARK IV Roller Die Cutting
  Machine
Accu-Cut Die-Cuts~Clear Cut Sun, large;
  Banner #3, large; Circle, large; Tulip
  #2, large; Flower, large; Rabbit #1B,
  small
Cotton Fabric
Assorted Buttons
Heat'n Bond Fusible Adhesive
Embroidery Floss
ZIG Memory System Markers~
  Millennium: Black 03

SCHOOL ALBUM COVER

Design by Jean Kievlan for Accu-Cut

TECHNIQUES

Die-Cut - Fabric
Lettering

MATERIALS

Accu-Cut MARK IV Roller Die Cutting Machine
Accu-Cut Die-Cuts~Schoolhouse, large; Deckle;
    Rectangle #1, large; Mini Apples
Black Spiral Bound album
Xyron 850 Machine
Xyron 850 Acid-Free Adhesive Cartridge
Cotton Blend Fabric~1/4 yard each color
ZIG Memory System Marker~White Opaque, Extra Fine
Jute Twine
3/8" Gold Liberty Bell

LET'S EAT

Design from Fiskars, Inc.

TECHNIQUES

Textures - Crimping
Matting

MATERIALS

Fiskars Personal Paper Trimmer
Fiskars Paper Crimper
Paper Pizazz Papers~Country, Solid
Jewel Tones

GOING BUGGY

Design by Sandra Cashman for Fiskars, Inc.

TECHNIQUES

Textures - Crimping
Cutting - Silhouette
Cutting - Circle Cutter
Journaling

MATERIALS

Fiskars:
 Circle Cutter and Mat
 Paper Edgers~Scallop
 Hand Punch~Teardrop
 Paper Crimper
Paper Pizazz Papers~Disney Classics; Dots,
    Checks, Plaids & Stripes; Plain Pastels
Brads (Don't use with original photos.)

RAFFIA WRAPPED FRAME

Design by Kathy Peterson for Memory Magic

TECHNIQUE
3-Dimensional

MATERIALS
Walnut Hollow Wood Frame
Folk Art Paints~Berry Wine
Raffia Accents~Golden Natural,
   Burgundy

MONOGRAMMED WEDDING FRAME

Design by Diane Bantz for Delta Technical Coatings

TECHNIQUES
Stenciling - Foil
Textures - Faux Finish

MATERIALS
5" x 7" Ceramic Frame
Delta:
   Crackle Medium
   Ceramcoat Acrylic Paint~Light Ivory
   Ceramcoat Gleam~14K Gold
   Satin Interior Spray Varnish
   Monogram Magic Gold Foiling Kit
   Monogram Magic Sentiment Stencil
      (appropriate letter)

HENRY DOORLY ZOO

Design by Linda Ullrich for Accu-Cut

TECHNIQUES

Rubber Stamping - Die-Cuts
Creative Cutting - Torn Paper
Journaling - Computer

MATERIALS

Accu-Cut MARK IV Roller Die Cutting Machine
Accu-Cut Die-Cuts~Lizard, small; Elephant #2,
    small; Clear Cut Rectangle, large
Circle Punch~1/16"
Rubber Stamp Starter Set
ZIG Memory System Markers~Writer
Paper Pizazz Papers~Green, Tan Flecked
Cardstock~Green, Tan
Ink Pad~Brown
Feather
Hemp~Green

SEPTEMBER & CORINA

Design by Sarah Fishburn for Memory Makers

TECHNIQUES
Rubber Stamping
Journaling - Computer
Cutting and Layering

MATERIALS
Paper Pizazz Papers~Dark Green, Medium
    Blue, Ivory with Green Leaves, Ivory
Stamps~Butterfly, Flower
Ink Pad~Burgundy
Colored chalks

TEDDY BABY CARD

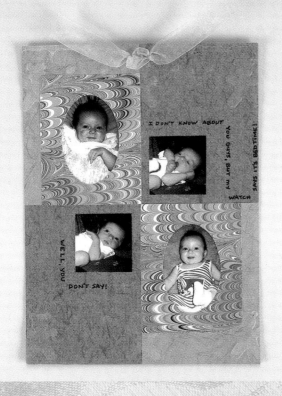

Design by Linda Ullrich for Accu-Cut

TECHNIQUES

Embossing - Pressure
Journaling
Die-Cuts

MATERIALS

Accu-Cut MARK IV Roller Die
    Cutting Machine
Accu-Cut Die-Cuts~Oval Picture
    Frame, large; Border Teddy Bear,
    long cut
Roller Embossing System
Circle Punch
ZIG Memory System Markers~Writer
Cardstock~Black
Paper Pizazz Papers~Purple, Pink,
    Marbled

HAPPY HOLIDAYS CARD

Design by Toni Nelson for EK Success

TECHNIQUES

Borders & Corners - Template
Lettering
Embossing - Markers

MATERIALS

Border Buddy~Winter
ZIG Memory System Embossing
    Markers~Writer
Embossing Powders~White
Vellum Paper

FALL LEAVES

Design from Fiskars, Inc.

TECHNIQUES	MATERIALS
Texture - Brayer, Crimping	Paper Pizazz Papers~Gold, Olive Green, Rust, Fall Leaf
Die-Cuts	Fiskars:
	Brayer~Mesh Design
	Corner Edgers~Rounder
	Paper Crimper
	ZIG Memory System Marker~Writer: Dark Green
	Accu-Cut Die-Cut~Leaf

STICKERS, PUNCH-OUTS & PAPER DOLLS

7

You'll have hours of fun just choosing which stickers or punch-outs to use to embellish your memory pages.

STICKER OPTIONS

Stickers are available in such a wide variety that you can match just about any theme and style. They fill in empty space and help carry out the theme of your page. Make sure the stickers you use are acid-free. Stickers can be used for borders, accents, corner mounts, replacing letters or words, or can even used to create an entire scene. Stickers can also help cover up a mistake—don't forget to add a few more, so it's not obvious. However, as a rule, be conservative when using stickers. Too many can take away from your photos.

JOURNALING

You'll add character to a page by using stickers to replace letters in words, or words in sentences. Have the kids help with this...it'll be loads of fun. (See Super Dad on page 92) Use stickers that are quotes or phrases, adding a little humor to your scrapbooking.

CUTTING AND LAYERING

Cut stickers and use them in and around pictures, mats, borders, etc. Add dimension by overlapping stickers, such as hanging the cowboy hat on the arm of a cactus. (See Little Buckaroos on page 92)

Tip: When you only want part of a sticker to stick: Use a cotton swab to pick up a small amount of baby powder, and apply to the backside of the sticker where you do not wish it to adhere. This will neutralize the adhesive.

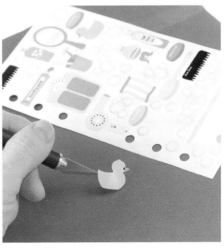

Use Fiskars Softgrip Razor Knife to apply small stickers easily.

PUNCH-OUTS

Place your stickers on wax paper and lay it over your page. You can move them around until you get the look you want, and you won't ruin your page. This is also a great way to evenly space letters for a title or name.

FRAMES

When you want to use only a couple of photos but want to really play them up, frame them! These frames are so easy to use—just punch out and slip on top of your photo. They're even pre-matted so your photos stand out from background papers. Because they're not adhesive, you can move them around your page to find the perfect placement before gluing them.

CARDS

For a great gift, choose a memory card all ready to insert your photo and send. Many come with punch-outs to accent your photo and tie it in with the card.

EMBELLISHMENTS

These punch-outs are a little like die-cuts and something like stickers. Some of the punch-out designs available include generic, themed and even licensed art, such as Disney characters. All you do is punch and glue. Beautifully detailed images are perfect for decorating your album pages. They're acid-free and sold in theme books.

Punch-Outs are an easy way to embellish your page with color and style.

PAPER DOLLS

There is an entire world of paper dolls and accessories out there just waiting to be placed in your scrapbooks. Using matching paper doll punch-outs lets you highlight all kinds of sports, hobbies, and personality types! Selecting the doll's hair color to match the photos pulls all of the elements together. You can design and create your own wardrobe for the dolls using the purchased clothing accessories for templates, decorative papers or fabrics, and paper edgers.

FAMILY TREE

Here's a great idea. Create your family tree in your scrapbook using paper dolls for each member of the family. Match hair and eye color to each person and dress the dolls similarly to the way their corresponding family member dresses.

Paper dolls can be created using punch-outs, templates, or a die-cutting system.

PUNCH ART

Punch Art is created using the smaller punches for individual shapes. It is easier than hand cutting shapes like flowers, hearts, and stars, and more versatile than stickers, giving you the option of choosing your own paper colors and prints. It's easy to assemble intricate looking creations, using simple shapes as the basic elements for your design.

LITTLE BUCKAROOS

Design by Jennie Dayley for EK Success

TECHNIQUES

Stickers - Layering, Replacing letters
Creative Cutting - Torn Paper
Lettering

MATERIALS

Stickopotamus Stickers~Cowboy
ZIG Memory System Markers~
    Scroll and Brush: Brown;
    Calligraphy: Brown; Writer:
    Black
Cardstock~Tan, Brown

MY SUPER DAD

Design by Jennie Dayley for EK Success

TECHNIQUES

Stickers - Journaling
Journaling - Lettering

MATERIALS

Stickopotamus Stickers~Morning
    Commute
ZIG Memory System Marker~
    Writer: Navy
Paper Pizazz Papers~Slate, Textured
    Background Papers

LET'S BOWL

Design by Toni Nelson for EK Success

TECHNIQUES
Borders & Corners - Template
Stickers
Journaling

MATERIALS
Border Buddy Jr.~Reflections
ZIG Memory System Markers~Writer:
 Pure Black; Calligraphy: Pure Black;
 Fine & Chisel: Salmon
Stickopotamus Stickers~Bowling
Paper Pizazz Papers~Pink, Green

FALL FLING

Design by Toni Nelson for EK Success

TECHNIQUES
Borders & Corners - Template
Stickers

MATERIALS
Border Buddy~Snapshots
ZIG Memory System Markers~Fine & Chisel:
 Pure Orange; Writer: Pure Brown,
 Summer Sun
Stickopotamus Stickers~Fall Leaves
Paper Pizazz Papers~Orange, Yellow

FUN IN THE SUN

Design by Toni Nelson for EK Success

TECHNIQUES
Embossing - Pressure
Borders - Template
Matting
Stickers
Lettering

MATERIALS
Border Buddy~Beach
Embossing Stylus
ZIG Memory System Markers~Writer: Splash
Stickopotamus Stickers~Pool
Paper Pizazz Papers~Solid Brights, Plain Pastels
Fiskars Paper Trimmer

MY BEST FRIEND

Design by Gordon Wells for Ticker's Stickers

TECHNIQUES

Stickers
Creative Cutting - Torn Paper
Dimensional - Dots
Matting
Journaling

MATERIALS

Paper Pizazz Papers~Colors to compliment photos
Gold Embossed Class A Peels~Hearts, Wedding
    Bells, Doves, Numbers
ZIG Memory System Markers~Writer: Pure Gold,
    Black 03
Dimensional Dots
EK Success Circle Ruler

ANIMAL KINGDOM

Design by Gordon Wells for Ticker's Stickers

TECHNIQUES
Borders & Corners - Template
Dimensional - Dots

MATERIALS
Paper Pizazz Papers~Solid Muted Colors
Border Buddy Jr.~Square Dance
Border Buddy~Snapshots
Dimensional Dots

ANITA, TERESA, ELSA

Design by Bernice Wery for Hot Off the Press

Spring 1999

Anita Teresa Elsa

TECHNIQUES

Matting
Punches

MATERIALS

Paper Pizazz Papers~Perfect Pairs: Yellow
   & Black; Solids: Perfect Pairs
Fiskars Paper Edgers~Colonial, Deckle
ZIG Memory System Marker~Writer
Maple Leaf Punch

"MOLLY 1998" CARD

Design from Hot Off The Press

TECHNIQUES
Cards - Punch-Outs
Lettering

MATERIALS
Rainbow Hearts Card
Fiskars Paper Edgers~Victorian
ZIG Memory System Marker~Writer: Magenta

SCHOOL CLASS PHOTO

Design by Carol Snyder for EK Success

TECHNIQUES
Paper Dolls
Journaling - Lettering

MATERIALS
Paper Pizazz Papers~Blue, Yellow,
    Brown
EK Success Paperkins~A+ Abby
ZIG Memory System Markers~Writer:
    Black; Opaque Writer: White,
    fine tip; Millennium: Black 01, 03
Fiskars Paper Edgers~Zipper

PARTY BOX

Design by Carol Snyder for EK Success

TECHNIQUES
Paper Dolls
Stickers
Lettering

MATERIALS
Paper Pizazz Papers~Purple, Lime Green
EK Success Paperkins~Patrick Party,
    Celebrating Cindy
ZIG Memory System Markers~Writer:
    Pink; Opaque Writer: White;
    Millennium: Black 03
Stickopotamus Stickers~Balloons on roll
Fiskars Paper Edgers~Pinking

DOLLS IN OUTFITS

Design by Kim McCrary for Creating Keepsakes Magazine

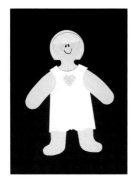

TECHNIQUES
Paper Dolls
Stickers
Stamping
Punches

MATERIALS
Accu-Cut Paper Dolls
Stampendous! Face Stamp
Paper Pizazz Papers
Fiskars Paper Edgers~Seagull
Punches~Circle, Flower, Heart, Swirl,
    Snowflake, Daisy, Flower corner,
    Cloud, Star, Rectangles
Stickopotamus Stickers

HAPPY MEMORIES STORAGE BOX

Design by Andrea Rothenberg for Highsmith

TECHNIQUES

Paper Dolls
Die-Cuts
Dimensional - Folding Flowers, Dots
Texture - Paper Crimping
Lettering

MATERIALS

Highsmith Acid-Free Corruboard Hinged Top Storage Box
Acid-Free Corruboard Craft Sheet
Delta Cherished Memories Acid-Free Paper Paint~Baby Blue
Accu-Cut Die Cuts~Paper Dolls, Doll Hair, Doll Clothes of choice, small
    Nested Flowers, large; Grass Border
Zig Memory System Markers~Scroll and Brush: Assorted Colors
Fiskars Paper Crimper
Dimensional Dots

SPORTS STARS

Design by
Bernice Wery for Hot Off the Press

TECHNIQUES
Punch-Outs - Paper Dolls
Matting
Journaling

MATERIALS
Paper Pizazz Papers~Metallic: Metallic
    Stars, Silver Metallic; Solid
    Muted: Yellow, Cream
Paper Pizazz Punch-Outs~Paper Dolls
Fiskars Paper Edgers~Pinking,
    Mountain Peaks
ZIG Memory System Marker~Writer

BALLET RECITAL

Design by Bernice Wery for Hot Off the Press

TECHNIQUES
Punch-Outs - Paper Dolls
Matting
Journaling

MATERIALS
Paper Pizazz Papers~Pretty: Pink Satin;
    Solid Muted: Green, Purple
Paper Pizazz Punch-Outs~Paper Dolls
Fiskars Paper Edgers~Ripple, Scallop
ZIG Memory System Marker~Clean Color
Leaf Punch

8 MEMORABILIA

You don't have to limit your memories to items that can lay flat on a scrapbook page. Get creative and incorporate all of your keepsakes in your memory books and projects.

MEMORABILIA POCKETS

With archival-safe memorabilia pockets, you can include memorabilia like baby hair, jewelry, concert tickets, etc. anywhere in your scrapbook. They come in a variety of sizes and have expandable pockets and a removable adhesive flap to keep important memories safe and secure.

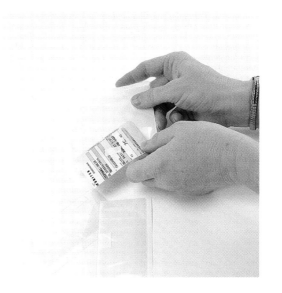

Use acid-free memorabilia pockets for items that can't be glued to your scrapbook page.

SHADOWBOXES

A shadowbox is a unique way to show off a group of 3-dimensional keepsakes while keeping them safe from dust and little hands. Create a display using a combination of photos and memorabilia. Pull it all together by matching background paint or fabrics to the colors of the items.

RECIPES

Scrapbooking can be a wonderful way to preserve family recipes. Those hand-me-down recipes can be color copied to show the spatters and spills from your ancestors' kitchens. Then they are safe to include right on your memory page. Or you can preserve original handwritten notes that really capture personality as well as history. Create nostalgic pieces of your past by safely storing them in an envelope or pocket and keeping them with the memory photos.

Tip: For those brittle papers at risk of falling apart: Spray with deacidifying spray, place on buffered paper and store in a clear Mylar sleeve. This won't reverse deterioration but will stop it.

POCKET PAGES

Do you save everything? Cards, notes, letters, artwork, receipts, ticket stubs, programs, travel brochures...anything related to memories? It's wonderful when you can incorporate these items into your memory pages, but it's not always easy or pretty. You can still include them with the memory, safely tucked away and easily accessible. All you need is a pocket. There are several ways you can create a place to store your memorabilia on the page and still make it an attractive layout. You're also keeping your photos safe from items that might not be acid-free.

Tip: When making pocket pages, it is necessary to trim about 1/4" from one side of your album page.

FULL PAGE POCKET

Adhere two pages together on the right, left and bottom sides and cut a few inches off the top of the top page to make an opening for the contents to peek through. Get creative with the design, coordinating it with the theme of your page—embellish with borders, stickers, scalloped edges or stenciling. You might even cut out a window, attaching clear Mylar to the inside, making sure everyone knows there's more to see.

CUSTOM-SIZE POCKET

Cut rectangle (or desired shape) from heavy paper. Glue three sides of rectangle to bottom of page to create a pocket. Decorate to match rest of page.

BOXES

When you have larger memorabilia or items that just can't go in an envelope or pocket, why not decorate a box that's photo safe? This is great for over-size kids' projects and artwork.

MILITARY MEMORIES SHADOWBOX

Design by Sandy Laipply for Memory Magic

TECHNIQUE
Shadowbox
Faux Painting

MATERIALS
11" x 14" shadowbox
Delta Ceramcoat Paints~Avocado,
   Sandstone, Maple Sugar Tan

Delta:
   Crackle Finish
   Wood Sealer
   Stitchless Fabric Glue
   Matte Varnish
Paintbrush~1"
Small scraps of foamboard
11" x 14" fabric scrap

TRAVEL TREASURES KEEPSAKE BOX/CHEST

Design by Mary Lynn Maloney for Memory Magic

TECHNIQUES
Rubber Stamping

MATERIALS
2" x 5" x 7" Papier Maché Hinged-lid Box
Vintage postage stamps
Rubber Stamps~Toy Box, Tin Can Mail
Stamp pad
Key charm
Grosgrain ribbon
Felt squares
Circle Punch
Paper fasteners~Six 3/4"
Paper~White, Orange, Dark Blue, Brown

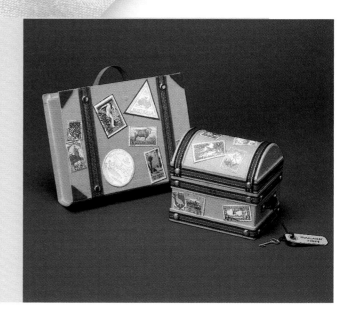

EASTER MEMORIES JOURNAL

Design by Alice Disney Huelskamp for Delta Technical Coatings

TECHNIQUES
Stenciling - Sponges
Journaling

MATERIALS
Delta:
 Stencil Sponges
 Stencil Buddy
 Archival Quality Photo-Safe Glue
 Borders & More! Stencils~Whimsical Dot
  Alphabet
 Cherished Memories Acid-Free Paper
  Paint~Baby Blue, Breezy Lilac, Garden
  Green, Orange Sizzle, Petal Pink, White

MONOGRAMMED BOX

Design by Nancy Olson for Delta Technical Coatings

TECHNIQUES
Stenciling - Foil

MATERIALS
Delta:
 Monogram Magic Monogram Stencils
 Self-Adhesive Reusable Stencil
 Stencil Buddy
 Renaissance Foil~Silver
 Renaissance Foil Adhesive
 Ceramcoat Acrylic Paint~Seashell White
 Exterior/Interior Matte Varnish
 1" Magic Tape
Hexagon papier machè box

SPECIAL OCCASION KEEPSAKE BOX

Design by Andrea Rothenberg for Highsmith

TECHNIQUES

Matting

Journaling - Computer

MATERIALS

Highsmith Corruboard Acid-Free Keepsake
    Case

Paper Pizazz Papers~Handmade Look Acid-Free
    Paper

Fiskars Paper Edgers~Bat Wings

Fiskars Corner Edgers~Nostalgia

FILM CREW

Design by Julie McGuffee for Pioneer

TECHNIQUES	MATERIALS
Photo Corners	Pioneer Album Paper
Memorabilia	Pioneer Photo Corners~Rainbow
Matting - Silhouette	Pioneer Photo Memory Mounting Paper
	Paper Pizazz Papers~Mickey & Friends;
	Plain Brights

HANDS ON CRAFTS FOR KIDS

Design by Julie McGuffee for Pioneer

TECHNIQUES

Pocket Page
Borders & Corners - Template
Journaling

MATERIALS

Pioneer Album Refill Paper
Pioneer Photo Corners~Rainbow
Pioneer Photo Memory Mounting Tape
Paper Pizazz Papers~Magic Kingdom
ZIG Memory System Marker~Writer
Border Buddy~Snapshots
Fiskars Paper Edgers~Pinking, Corkscrew, wide

FRUIT SALAD, ANYONE?

Design from Fiskars, Inc.

Grannie's Fruit Topping
3 egg yolks
2 tsp. Powdered sugar
1/3 cup white wine (sweet)
Grated lemon
1/3 cup Cool Whip

Whip egg yolks w/sugar until nic...
double broiler and whip whil...
peel. When cool, stir in C...

TECHNIQUES

Pocket Pages - Custom
Creative Cutting - Ovals
Die-Cuts
Journaling - Computer

MATERIALS

Fiskars:
   Oval Cutter and Mat
   Corner Edgers~Blossom
   Hand Punch~Teardrop
   Paper Edgers~Seagull, wide
   Portable Paper Trimmer
   Paper Pizazz Papers~Florals; Dots, Checks,
      Plaids & Stripes; Brights
   Accu-Cut Die-Cuts~Circles, Ribbon

RECIPES

Design by LeNae Gerig for Memory Makers

Helen Olivia Stacy Adams

Grandma Adams made the best Corn chowder in the county. After she passed away, I found her hand written recipe and made a batch myself. When he tasted it ,Dad said it brought back memories of sitting in the kitchen on winter days while Grandma cooked.

Corn Chowder
3 cups Whole Kernal Corn
5 cups diced potatoes

TECHNIQUES	MATERIALS
Pocket Pages	Paper Pizazz Papers~Antique Lace, Tan, Brown
Matting	Paper Pizazz Punch-Outs~Watercolor
Photo Corners	Fiskars Photo Corners~Black
Journaling - Computer	Fiskars Paper Edgers~Deckle
Punch-Outs	

FAVORITE FAMILY RECIPE BOOK

Design by Jennie Dayley for EK Success

MATERIALS

Stickopotamus Stickers~Baking, Tropical, Rainy Day, BBQ, Ice Cream, Cakes, Traffic, Ice Cream, Camping, Garden, Morning Commute, Scrapbook

ZIG Memory System Markers~Calligraphy: Blue Jay; Writer: Black, Yellow, Pure Blue, Pure Red, Brown, Pure Pink, Blue Jay, Spring Green; Fine & Chisel: Pure Red, Pure Pink; Scroll and Brush: Red

TECHNIQUES

Stickers
Journaling - Lettering
Memorabilia - Recipes

PROM FUN

Design by Tammy Muto for 3-L

TECHNIQUES

Photo Corners
Memorabilia Pockets
Punches

MATERIALS

3L:
  Photo Corners~Clear
  Photo Fix Corners
  Memorabilia Pocket~Large Square
Paper Pizazz Papers~Solid Jewel Tones:
  Navy Blue, Grey
ZIG Memory System Markers~Opaque
  Writer: Gold
Stickers or Punches~Swirl; Stars
Fiskars Paper Edgers~Pisces

HOMECOMING 1999

Design by Tammy Muto for 3-L

TECHNIQUES

Photo Corners
Memorabilia Pockets
Journaling

MATERIALS

3L:
  Photo Corners~Black
  Photo Fix Corners
  Memorabilia Pocket
Paper Pizazz Papers~Metallic Papers Book
ZIG Memory System Markers~Opaque
  Writer: Gold
Fiskars Paper Edgers~Pisces

9 FUN WITH COMPUTERS

Computers can give you access to thousands of scrapbooking tips, layouts, and professional images. Using your computer to help you be more organized will allow more time for scrapbooking .

GENERAL TIPS

With a color printer, you can print clip art and text directly onto your scrapbook page.

How about hand coloring black and white print-outs to coordinate with the photos on your pages? You can either print directly onto acid-free paper and place directly in your scrapbook, or print onto acid-free paper and cut out the art to add to a page. The latter is a great way to use your computer for 12" x 12" pages or 3-D keepsakes.

ENLARGING/REDUCING

By using a computer, you can easily adjust the size of artwork, borders, and fonts so they balance with the other elements of your page. When you find a perfect die-cut for your layout but it's the wrong size, scan the die-cut into the computer and enlarge or reduce it to the right size. As mentioned in the journaling chapter, using your computer is the easiest way to adjust your lettering to fit your journaling space.

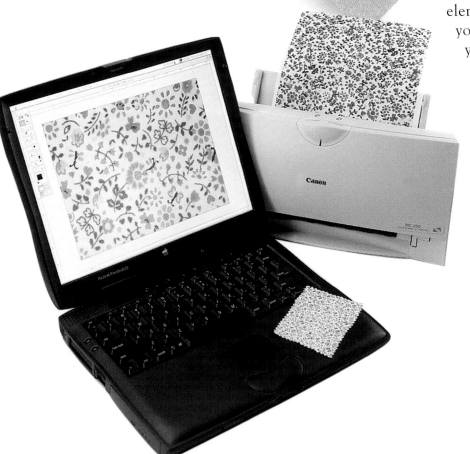

SCRAPBOOK SOFTWARE

Using the computer to help you create scrapbook images takes you far beyond the limits of materials available. Create unique papers, stickers, die-cuts, borders, and frames. Journaling becomes easier, with the ability to choose from many fonts and being able to adjust the size to fit your working area. This new and innovative software contains everything necessary to create a complete scrapbook page. You can digitally crop images with paper edgers, choose backgrounds from hundreds of

Fiskars Scrapware is just one of the many scrapbooking software packages available to help you create memory pages using your computer.

pre-designed layouts, get creative with thousands of pieces of clip art, and more. Scan, print, and resize photos and even eliminate images (red eye) you don't want in the photo. When shopping for software, use your computer as a resource: scrapbooking websites, chat rooms, and message boards will be great places to find software recommendations. See the front of the book for website addresses.

Use scrapbook software to create scrapbook pages, picture frames, cards, stationery, and more. Design a customized page to complement any photo. Designs are included so you can crop images right on the screen, complete with decorative edges and mats. Software often includes background designs, clip art, and numerous quotes and sayings. Import images from the Internet, too.

CLIP-ART

Software packages have clip-art available in black and white, color only, and some offer both formats. Look for programs that include a browser, allowing you to see all of the images in a "thumbnail" version, saving you time when searching for the right image. How about printing the clip-art onto sticker paper? Just cut it out and...instant stickers.

117

SCANNER

If you have a scanner for your home computer, the possibilities are endless for creating your own paper. You can scan just about anything—other paper, fabric, clothing, and even dimensional objects—print it and instantly, you have your own original design scrapbook paper. Here are just a few ideas of things to scan and create background papers from: wallpaper, baby blankets, toys, leaves, food (pasta noodles), items of clothing or newspapers.

Just about anything can be scanned and used to create unique background paper for your pages. Scan fabric to make colorful paper for mats and backgrounds.

PHOTOGRAPHS

Now you can even have your photographs in electronic format with the use of digital cameras and scanners. With the software available, once your images are on your computer, you can do just about anything from creating cards to calendars to electronic scrapbooks. It's easy to email or add your family memories to web sites and share them with your family and friends hundreds of miles away.

LAYOUTS

There are also software programs designed to help you lay out your scrapbook pages. Many of these include clip-art and fonts as well.

SEARCH TOOL

Use your search tool on the Internet to find all sorts of great stuff for scrapbooking. You can find clip-art, free fonts, great scrapbooking websites for tips and ideas, and even research your family's heritage.

RUB-A-DUB-DUB

Design from Fiskars, Inc.

TECHNIQUES
Computer - Software
Photo Corners - Custom

MATERIALS
Fiskars:
  Scrapware
  Swivel Knife
  Portable Paper Trimmer
  Photo Stickers

SMOCKED DRESS

Design by Julie McGuffee for Pioneer

Julie's 7th Birthday

TECHNIQUES

Scanning - Paper Making
Creative Cutting
Matting
Journaling

MATERIALS

Pioneer Album Refill Paper
Pioneer Photo Corners~Transparent
Paper Pizazz Papers~Pretty Papers; Solid Muted
  Colors
ZIG Memory System Marker~Calligraphy: Blue

SPRING INTO FALL

Design by Julie McGuffee for Pioneer

TECHNIQUES

Scanning - Paper Making
Cutting - Bumping Out

MATERIALS

Paper Pizazz Papers~Stripes, Checks and Dots
Pioneer Album Paper
Fiskars Paper Edgers~Corkscrew, wide

THE MEMORY EXPERTS

Carol Snyder
EK Success

Deanna Lambson and Stacy Jullian
Creating Keepsakes

Jean Kievlan
Accu-Cut

Rick Collies
Pioneer
Memory
Albums

122

Paulette Jarvey
Hot Off The Press

Hosts Julie Stephani and Julie McGuffee
Krause Publications

Tammy Muto
3-L and Delta Technical Coatings

Andrea
Rothenberg
Highsmith

Chris Taylor
Highsmith

Experts in scrapbooking joined hosts Julie Stephani and Julie McGuffee to tape the TV series More Than Memories at the David Larson Studios in Menomonee Falls, Wisconsin. The show features the latest in creative scrapbooking ideas and techniques. The show is available on Public Broadcasting Service television stations. Check your local PBS broadcasting schedule.

*Toni Nelson and Beth Reames
EK Success*

*Sandra Cashman - Fiskars, Inc.
Patti Swoboda - Jangle.com*

*Jennie Dayley
Stickopotamus*

*Host Julie with Michele Gerbrandt
Memory Makers*

BEHIND THE SCENES

Jill Rinner and C.J. Wilson
Accu-Cut

Host Julie with Gordon Wells
Ticker's Stickers, Inc.

Hosts Julie and
Julie with some
of the TV crew!

Alison Berquist
Ticker's Stickers, Inc.

125

GLOSSARY

ACID FREE

Acid is used in paper manufacturing to break apart the wood fibers and the lignin which holds them together. If acid remains in the materials used for photo albums, the acid can react chemically with photographs and accelerate their deterioration. Acid-free products have a pH factor of 7 to 8.5. It's imperative that all materials (glue, pens, paper, etc.) used in memory albums or scrapbooks be acid free.

ACID MIGRATION

Acid migration is the transfer of acidity from one item to another through physical contact or acidic vapors. If a newspaper clipping was put into an album, the area it touched would turn yellow or brown. A de-acidification spray can be used on acidic paper or they can be color photocopied onto acid-free papers.

BUFFERED PAPER

During manufacturing a buffering agent such as calcium carbonate or magnesium bicarbonate can be added to paper to neutralize acid contaminants. Such papers have a pH of 8.5.

CROPPING

Cropping is cutting or trimming a photo to keep only the most important parts.

DIE CUTS

Precut paper shapes used to decorate pages.

JOURNALING

Journaling refers to the text on an album page giving details about the photographs. It can be done in your own handwriting or with adhesive letters, rub-ons, etc. It is one of the most important parts of memory albums because it tells the story behind the photos.

MATTING

Background paper used to frame and enhance the photo image.

pH FACTOR

The pH factor refers to the acidity of a paper. The pH scale is the standard for measurement of acidity and alkalinity. It runs from 0 to 14 with each number representing a tenfold increase. pH neutral is 7. Acid-free products have a pH factor from 7 to 8.5. Special pH tester pens are available to help determine the acidity or alkalinity of products.

PHOTO SAFE

This is a term similar to "archival quality" but more specific to materials used with photographs. Acid-free is the determining factor for a product to be labeled photo safe.

SHEET PROTECTORS

These are made of plastic to slip over a finished album page. They can be side-loading or top-loading. It is important that they be acid free. Polypropylene is commonly used. Never use vinyl sheet protectors.

Reprinted from *Making Great Scrapbook Pages*, Hot Off The Press, Inc.

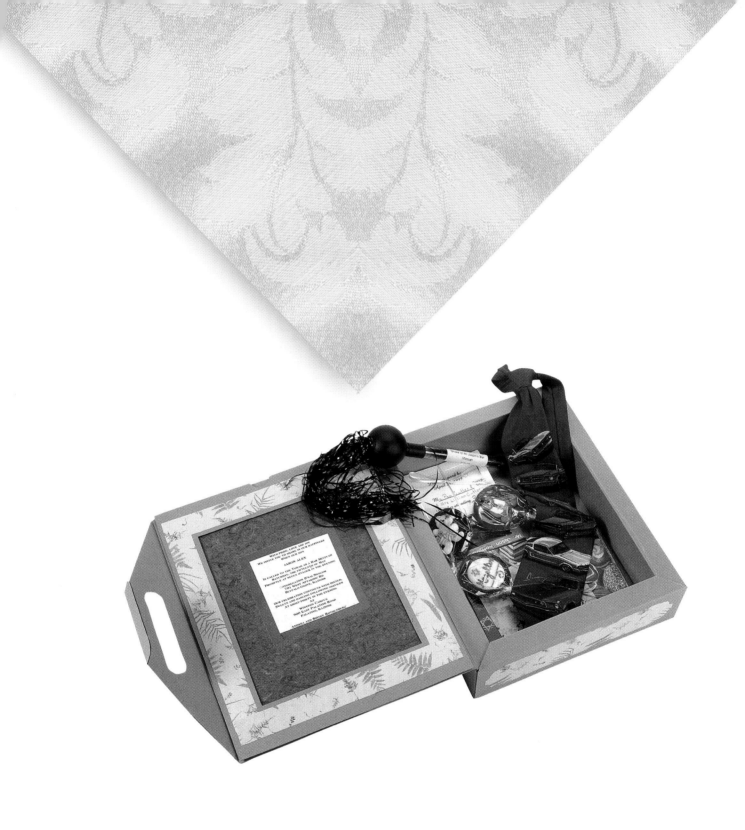